Contents

INTRODUCTION..
WHAT IS TAE KWON DO 3
GRADING SYSTEM AND BELT COLOUR 3
STANCES – SOGI 9
SAJU JIRUGI 14
SAJU MAKI 20
GRADING 27
CHON JI 29
TENETS OF TAE KWON DO (Tae Kwon Do Jungshin) 37
RULES OF THE DOJANG 39
MOVES SPECIFIC TO DAN GUN 40
DAN GUN 42
MOVES SPECIFIC TO DO SAN 50
DO SAN 52
ATTACKING TECHNIQUES *(Gong Gyoki)* 63
KICKING TECHNIQUES 64
MOVES SPECIFIC TO WON HYO 66
WON HYO 68
MOVES SPECIFIC TO YUL GOK 78
YUL GOK 81
MISCELLANEOUS TERMS AND DEFINITIONS 95
MOVES SPECIFIC TO JOONG GUN 98
JOONG GUN 102
MOVES SPECIFIC TO TOI GYE 114
TOI GYE 117
POWER 131
MOVES SPECIFIC TO HWA RANG 134
HWA RANG 137
MOVES SPECIFIC TO CHOONG MOO 149
CHOONG MOO 152

Mobile: 0742 33 33 007

INTRODUCTION

We are a group called *"Elite Tae Kwon Do Scotland"*, headed by Master Divine (7th Dan) & Mr Dutton (6th Dan). Established in 2001, we are one of the most successful groups in Scotland.

It is our mission to teach and promote ITF Tae Kwon Do in its true and Traditional form, free from politics. All our Instructors are fully certified, experienced, have full Indemnity insurance and are registered under the PVG Scheme.

Our schools adhere to strict guidelines and procedures ensuring a high standard in which we teach. Over the years, Elite have established a reputation built upon our standard of excellence.

We have classes especially designed for Children and separate Adult classes. Some venues however, offer Adults and Children's classes, these run simultaneously with our Senior Instructors. This is our most popular as many Parents wish to train alongside their Children.

If you wish to keep up to date with all our latest learning programs, please follow us on our social networking site below & also subscribe to our new YouTube channel.

www.youtube.com/theelitetaekwondo or
Facebook: Elite Taekwon Do Scotland

Web: www.elitetkd.uk

This series of books are designed to give students an understanding of Tae Kwon Do from starting your first class through to Black Belt grade and beyond. Whilst there is a lot of information, students are not expected to remember everything, especially in the early stages, however, as the student progresses, their knowledge should also progress. Each book covers the relevant patterns for that particular belt. These guides are designed to be used in conjunction with attending classes on a regular basis. It may be difficult to learn a new pattern in a class due to the number or complexity of moves. If the class has just had a grading, there may be many students ready to learn a new pattern and the instructor may not have enough time in the class to teach every move in detail. The instructor should ensure that time is spent going over new patterns but ultimately, it may be down to the student to research the pattern to learn the basic moves, the instructor, or senior student, can then refine the pattern in the class.

Other information regarding getting started, rules, tenets, power and Korean as well as descriptions of the various moves are described in detail within the books. By having the set of coloured belt books, the student should have the required information to successfully grade to black belt.

This guide has been compiled and written by Mr Stuart Dutton (VI Dan), an International instructor and examiner who has over 25 years experience of training and instructing and Mr Ian Kirkpatrick (V Dan), an instructor with over 15 years experience.

White Book 10th Kup / 9th Kup

Getting started
Grading format
Saju Jirugi / Saju Makgi / Chon Ji

Yellow Book 8th Kup / 7th Kup
Tenets of Tae Kwon Do
Instructor / student rules
Health and Safety
Dan Gun / Do San

Green Book 6th Kup / 5th Kup
Korean translation
Won hyo / Yul Gok

Blue Book 4th Kup / 3rd Kup
Miscellaneous terms and definitions
Joong Gun / Toi Gye

Red Book 2nd Kup / 1st Kup
Power
Hwa Rang / Choong Moo

WHAT IS TAE KWON DO

Tae Kwon Do can be translated as Tae (Foot), Kwon (Hand), Do (Way or art). Tae Kwon Do therefore translates as *"A method of self-defence using foot and hand techniques"*.

Tae Kwon Do was officially recognized as a Martial art on the 11th April 1955, its founder being General Choi Hong Hi, Black Belt 9th Dan and Grand Master of Tae Kwon Do. He was a Major General in the Korean Army and was responsible for the spreading of Tae Kwon Do to the Korean forces. It is a National sport in Korea and is taught in many of the universities and schools. On the 22nd Of March 1966, the International Tae Kwon Do Federation was formed with General Choi Hong Hi as President, having associations in Vietnam, Malaysia, Singapore, West Germany, USA, Turkey, Italy, United Arab Republic and Korea.

To the serious student of Tae Kwon Do it represents not merely the skilful use of foot and hand but a way of thinking and life, particularly in installing a spirit of self imposed discipline and developing self-confidence. In these days where violence and intimidation are everyday occurrences, Tae Kwon Do enables the student to possess a fine weapon to defend themselves. Through training, a student develops self-confidence, self-discipline, physical fitness, co-ordination and self-defence. It is an art not only for the strong but for any person wishing to be taught the art, young or old, male or female, big or small.

GRADING SYSTEM AND BELT COLOUR

Students are promoted in Tae Kwon Do after being successful in their grading examinations, which they are allowed to sit after having trained and studied for the required amount of time. Students start as a white belt and as they attend and pass a grading, are promoted to the next level. Students should attend a grading when they are confident that they have the required knowledge and ability. It is recognised that not all students will have the required ability or flexibility to complete certain moves, especially some of the high level kicks. This should be taken into account by the examiner who should grade the student on their individual ability.

Coloured Belt Grades and explanation of the belt

WHITE   Signifies the innocence of the beginning student who has no previous knowledge of Tae Kwon Do.

10th Kup

9th Kup

YELLOW   Signifies the earth from which the plant takes root and sprouts as Tae Kwon Do foundation is laid.

8th Kup   7th Kup

GREEN   Signifies the plants growth as Tae Kwon Do skills begin to develop.

6th Kup   5th Kup

BLUE   Signifies the heaven towards which the plant matures into a towering tree as training in Tae Kwon Do progresses.

4th Kup   3rd Kup

RED   Signifies danger, cautioning the student to exercise control and warning the opponent away

2nd Kup   1st Kup

BLACK   Opposite of white therefore signifying maturity and proficiency in Tae Kwon Do. It also indicates the wearer's imperviousness to darkness and fear.

Black Belt ranking is then split into Dans and are distinguished by the number written on the belt in Roman Numerals. Black belt students have black edging along the bottom edge of the jacket. Senior grades that have attended an International Instructors course will also have a black stripe running the length of both the trouser legs and arms of the suit.

Once black belt is reached, students must wait certain time periods between gradings to ensure they are proficient to receive the next ranking. Black belts are also split into sections – novice, expert and master.

1st Degree (I)	
2nd Degree (II)	**Novice**
3rd Degree (III)	
4th Degree (IV)	
5th Degree (V)	**Expert**
6th Degree (VI)	
7th Degree (VII)	
8th Degree (VIII)	**Master**
9th Degree (IX)	

When addressing the instructor or any black belt, the following titles are used

1st to 3rd Degree	Assistant Instructor (*Boosabum*)
4th to 6th Degree	Instructor (*Sabum*)
7th to 8th Degree	Master (*Sahyun*)
9th Degree	Grand Master (*Sasung*)

Getting started in the class

On first starting the class, loose comfortable clothing can be worn. A suit *(Dobok)* can be purchased through the club and should be worn with the correct colour of belt. As you progress, other items or equipment can be purchased. Hand and foot pads are essential to ensure safety whilst sparring. A mouth guard may also be advisable to prevent accidental injury.
Personal insurance should also be considered and can be purchased through the club although it may be mandatory. Each student may also have to purchase a yearly licence or registration. Elite students must have a licence and insurance to train and to sit gradings. There may also be a selection of promotional items available through your club, should you wish to purchase them. To gain an idea of prices or items available, these are displayed on our club web site:
www.elitetkd.uk

Students should arrive at the class early. On entering the training hall (*Dojang*), students should stop at the doorway or entrance and bow towards the class. Similarly, when leaving, the student should turn and bow towards the class.

To start the class, students form up in lines, the most senior student stands at the front right hand corner with junior students lining up to his left. Once that line is full, the next student stands at the right hand side, directly behind the senior student, with junior students to their left. Once the class is ready, the senior student will call the class to attention (*Charyot Sogi*) and then bow to the instructor, who will be standing at the front of the class

(*Charyot sogi* - feet are together, body upright, hands clenched and held out at belt level)

To start the class the senior rank says (assuming your instructor is IV to VI Degree)

Class Charyot	*Sabum Nimgeh*	*Kyong Ye*
Class Attention	Respect to the Instructor	Bow

If somebody else is taking the class then they would probably be I to III Degree and would be referred to as Boosabum

Class Charyot	*Boosabum Nimgeh*	*Kyong Ye*
Class Attention	Respect to the Instructor	Bow

If you are called upon to show respect to the senior rank rather than the instructor then the command will depend upon their rank. It could be either of the above if the senior rank is a black belt. If they are not a black belt then the command would be:

Class Charyot	*Kyong Ye*
Class Attention	Bow

Similarly, at the end of the class, the senior student will call the class to attention and bow to the instructor. The class will then face the senior student and the 2nd most senior student will call the class to attention and bow to the senior student. The senior rank then dismisses the class by raising their right hand and saying 'Hesan'

The students will then adopt parallel ready stance (*Narani Junbi Sogi*) and the class will begin. Each club will have different variations for training in class but should cover the main aspects of basic moves, patterns, sparring, special techniques and self defence. Kicking shields and focus pads may be used to practise kicking and striking.

(*Narani Junbi Sogi*- feet are shoulder width apart, facing forwards. Hands are clenched and held at belt level at the front of the body)

Four direction punch (Saji Jirugi) and four direction block (Saji Makgi) are the first two training exercises. Whilst they appear to be patterns, they are not classed as such.

Walking stance (*Gunnun Sogi*)

Feet are shoulder width apart and 1 ½ times shoulder width long. The front leg is bent slightly with the foot facing forward. The rear leg is straight with the foot turned slightly outwards. Weight is spread 50/50 on both legs.

Middle obverse punch *(baro jirugi)*

This is a punch to the centre of the body. The striking hand is brought back to the hip with the knuckles facing upwards. The other hand (reaction hand) is brought out to the front, knuckles facing the floor. As the punch is extended, the reaction hand is brought sharply back to the hip. Both hands twist so that the punch finishes with the knuckles facing the floor and the reaction hand ends on the hip, knuckles facing upwards. The body is upright and the shoulders are full facing.

Low outer forearm block (*najunde bakat palmok makgi*)

This is a low section block using the outer forearm (the part of the forearm on the pinkie side of the hand). The block starts with both hands crossed, level with the chest, the blocking hand closest to the body. The blocking hand has the knuckles facing the body and the reaction hand has the knuckles facing away from the body (back fist to back fist). As the blocking hand is brought down, the hand twists so that the hand finishes with the knuckles facing the floor. The arm is bent slightly and the body is upright, half facing. A knife hand block is executed in the same manner but the hand is opened at the moment of impact.

Full facing means that when the move is complete, the shoulders, when viewed from the side, are level and the body is fully facing the target. Half facing is when the leading shoulder is slightly forwards causing the body to be at an angle to the target.

Middle inner forearm block (*kaunde anpalmok makgi*)

This block uses the part of the forearm on the thumb side of the arm. The block starts with hands crossed, level with the chest, the blocking hand furthest from the body. Both back fists are facing the body. As the blocking hand is brought round, the hand twists so that it finishes with knuckles facing upwards, arm slightly bent. The reaction hand twists back onto the hip.

STANCES – SOGI

Basic Principles for a correct stance are:

1. Keep the back straight, with few exceptions
2. Relax the shoulders
3. Tense the abdomen
4. Maintain correct facing. The stance may be full facing, half facing or side facing the opponent.
5. Maintain equilibrium
6. Make proper use of the knee spring

Attention stance (charyot sogi)

This is an attention position used before and after each exercise.
Feet form a 45 degree angle
Drop the fists down naturally, bending the elbows slightly
The fists are clenched slightly
Eyes face the front slightly above the horizontal line

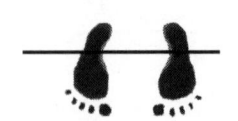

Closed stance (moa sogi)

Full facing or side facing
Body weight even on both feet

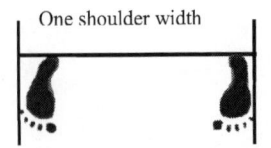

Parallel stance (narani sogi)

Spread the feet parallel to shoulder width
Keep the toes pointing towards the front
Full facing or side facing
Body weight even on both feet

Diagonal stance (sasun sogi)

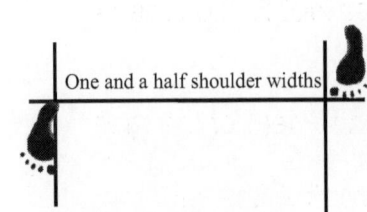

This is very useful for shifting into walking stance without relocating the foot. It is used for attacking or defending against the front or the rear.
Spread the legs to a distance of 1.5 shoulder widths between the big toes
The heel of the front foot is placed on the same line as the toes of

the rear foot
Point the toes to the front.
Body weight even on both feet
Extend the knees outward, bending until the knee caps come over the ball of the foot
Infuse the strength into the inner thighs and tense inward scraping the ground or floor with the side soles
Push both the chest and abdomen out and pull the hip tensing the abdomen
Full facing or side facing, in attack or defence
When the right foot is advanced it is a right stance, and vice versa

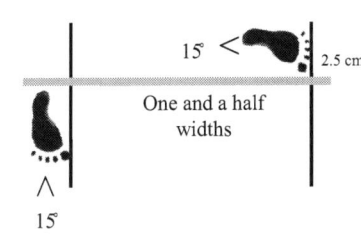

Fixed stance (gojung sogi)

It is an effective stance for attack and defence to the side.
Move one foot to either the front or rear a distance of 1.5 shoulder widths from the big toe of the rear foot to the toes of the front foot, almost forming a right angle
The toes of both feet point 15 degrees inward.
Place the heel of the front foot 2.5cm beyond the heel of the rear foot.
Bend the rear leg until the knee is aligned with the big toe, bending the front leg proportionally
Keep the hip aligned with the inner knee joint
Always half facing
Body weight even on both feet
When the right foot is advanced it is a right stance, and vice versa

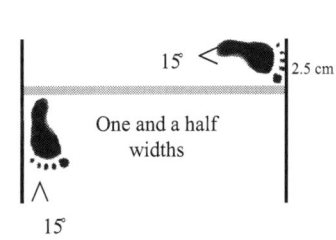

L stance (niunja sogi)

This is widely used in defence, though used in attack as well. The front leg is readily available for kicking with a slight shifting of the body weight and with the advantage of half facing as well as body shifting.
Move one foot to either the front or rear a distance of 1.5 shoulder widths from the foot sword of the rear foot to the toes of the front foot, almost forming a right angle.
The toes of both feet point 15° inward.
Place the heel of the front foot 2.5cm beyond the heel of the rear foot.
Bend the rear leg until the knee cap forms a vertical line with the

toes, bending the front leg proportionally
Keep the hip aligned with the inner knee joint
Always half facing
About 70 percent body weight on the rear leg and 30 percent on the front leg
When the right leg is bent it is a right stance, and vice versa
It is always half facing, both in attack and defence.

Low stance (nachuo sogi)

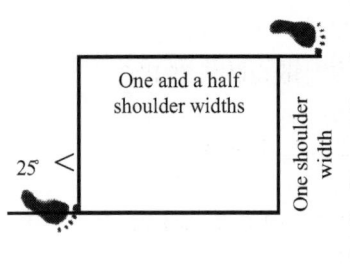

The advantage of this stance is the ease with which one can extend the attacking tool.
Move one foot to either the front or the rear at a distance of 1.5 shoulder widths between the big toe of the rear foot and the heel of the front foot, and 1 shoulder width apart from the centre of each instep.
Bend the front leg until the knee cap forms a vertical line with the heel, extending the opposite leg fully
Body weight even on both feet
Keep the toes of the front foot pointing forward, the opposite foot 25° outward.
When the right leg is bent it is a right stance, and vice versa
Full facing or half facing

Rear foot stance (dwitbal sogi)

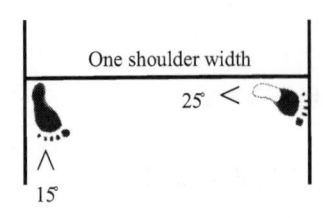

This is used for defence and occasionally for attack. The advantage of this stance is the ability to kick or adjust the distance from an opponent with the front foot, which can move spontaneously without any additional shifting of the body weight to the rear foot.
Move one foot either to the front or the rear a distance of 1 shoulder width between the small toes
Bend the rear leg until the knee comes over the toes, placing the heel
slightly beyond the heel of the front foot
Bend the front leg, touching the ground slightly with the ball of the foot
Keep the toes of the front foot 25o inward and the toes of the rear foot 15o inward.
Body weight mostly on the rear foot
When the right foot is in the rear it is a right stance, and vice versa
Be sure to keep the knee of the rear leg pointing slightly inwards

Sitting stance (annun sogi)

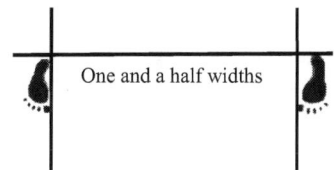

This is a very stable stance for lateral movement. It is also widely used for punching exercise and muscle development of the legs. One of the advantages of this stance is to shift into walking stance without relocating the foot.
Spread the legs to a distance of 1.5 shoulder widths between the big toes
Point the toes to the front.
Body weight even on both feet
Extend the knees outward, bending until the knee caps come over the ball of the foot
Infuse the strength into the inner thighs and tense inward scraping the ground or floor with the side soles
Push both the chest and abdomen out and pull the hip tense
Full facing or side facing, in attack or defence

Vertical stance (soojik sogi)

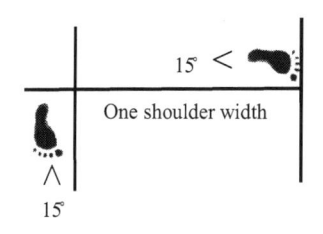

Move one foot to either the front or side a distance of 1 shoulder width between the big toes, almost forming a right angle
Keep the toes of both feet pointing 15o inward
Keep the legs straight
60 percent body weight on the rear leg and 40 percent on the front leg
When the right foot is in the rear it is a right stance, and vice versa
Always half facing

Walking stance (gunnun sogi)

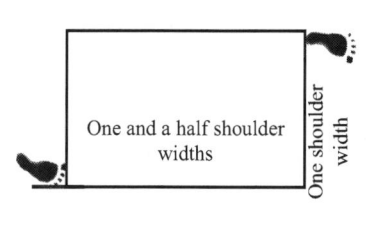

This is a strong stance for front and rear, both in attack and defence.
Move one foot to either the front or the rear at a distance of 1.5 shoulder widths between the big toes and 1 shoulder width apart from the centre of each instep.
Bend the front leg until the knee cap forms a vertical line with the heel, extending the opposite leg fully
Body weight even on both feet
Keep the toes of the front foot pointing forward, the opposite foot 25° outward.
Tense the muscles of the feet with the feeling of pulling them toward each other
When the right leg is bent it is a right stance, and vice versa
Full facing or half facing

X-stance (kyocha sogi)

This is a very convenient stance, in particular for attacking the side or front in a jumping motion. It is frequently used for blocking and serves as a preparatory stance for moving into the next manoeuvre.

Full, side or half facing in both attack and defence
Body weight on the stationary foot
When the weight is rested on the right foot it is a right stance, and vice versa
Cross one foot over or behind the other, touching the ground slightly with the ball of the foot
One foot always crosses over the front of the other with the exception of a jumping motion

Stepping   Jumping

SAJU JIRUGI

This is not classed as a pattern but is a training exercise to practise the basic moves.

Movements – 14

	Parallel ready Stance *Narani junbi Sogi* Feet shoulder width apart, toes facing forward. Fists clenched and held level with the belt.
	Walking stance middle obverse punch *Gunnan sogi baro jirugi* Stepping forward with the right foot into walking stance performing a mid section punch with the right hand, left hand on the hip.

Walking stance low outer forearm block
Gunnun sogi najunde bakat palmok makgi

Bring the right leg back to the left, turn to your left placing the right leg behind into a walking stance performing a low section block with the left outer forearm.

Walking stance middle obverse punch
Gunnan sogi baro jirugi

Stepping forward with the right foot into walking stance performing a mid section punch with the right hand, left hand on the hip.

Walking stance low outer forearm block
Gunnun sogi najunde bakat palmok makgi

Bring the right leg back to the left, turn to your left placing the right leg behind into a walking stance performing a low section block with the left outer forearm

Walking stance middle obverse punch
Gunnan sogi baro jirugi

Stepping forward with the right foot into walking stance performing a mid section punch with the right hand, left hand on the hip.

Walking stance low outer forearm block
Gunnun sogi najunde bakat palmok makgi

Bring the right leg back to the left, turn to your left placing the right leg behind into a walking stance performing a low section block with the left outer forearm

Walking stance middle obverse punch
Gunnan sogi baro jirugi

Stepping forward with the right foot into walking stance performing a mid section punch with the right hand, left hand on the hip.

Parallel ready Stance
Narani junbi Sogi

Bring the right leg back into parallel ready stance.

We now repeat this sequence of moves but moving in the opposite direction.

Walking stance middle obverse punch
Gunnan sogi baro jirugi

Stepping forward with the left foot into walking stance performing a mid section punch with the left hand, right hand on the hip.

Walking stance low outer forearm block
Gunnun sogi najunde bakat palmok makgi

Bring the left leg back to the right, turn to your right placing the left leg behind into a walking stance performing a low section block with the right outer forearm.

Walking stance middle obverse punch
Gunnan sogi baro jirugi

Stepping forward with the left foot into walking stance performing a mid section punch with the left hand, right hand on the hip.

Walking stance low outer forearm block
Gunnun sogi najunde bakat palmok makgi

Bring the left leg back to the right, turn to your right placing the left leg behind into a walking stance performing a low section block with the right outer forearm.

Walking stance middle obverse punch
Gunnan sogi baro jirugi

Stepping forward with the left foot into walking stance performing a mid section punch with the left hand, right hand on the hip.

Walking stance low outer forearm block
Gunnun sogi najunde bakat palmok makgi

Bring the left leg back to the right, turn to your right placing the left leg behind into a walking stance performing a low section block with the right outer forearm.

Walking stance middle obverse punch
Gunnan sogi baro jirugi

Stepping forward with the left foot into walking stance performing a mid section punch with the left hand, right hand on the hip.

Parallel ready Stance
Narani junbi Sogi

Bring the right leg back into parallel ready stance.

SAJU MAKI

This is the second of the training exercises for white belt and uses blocking techniques.

Movements – 16

	Parallel ready Stance *Narani Junbi Sogi* Standing with feet shoulder width apart, hands clenched and held at belt level.
	**Walking stance low knife hand block** *Gunnun sogi najunde sonkal makgi* Taking the right leg back to form a left walking stance, using the left hand to form a low knife hand block, bringing the right hand to the hip.
	**Walking stance middle inner forearm block** *Gunnun sogi kaunde anpalmok makgi* Stepping forward into a right walking stance, forming a middle side block with the right inner forearm, left hand on the hip.

Walking stance low knife hand block
Gunnun sogi najunde sonkal makgi

Turning to your left, bring your right leg back then place it out behind you to form a left walking stance, using the left hand to form a low knife hand block

Walking stance middle inner forearm block
Gunnun sogi kaunde anpalmok makgi

Stepping forward into a right walking stance, forming a middle side block with the right inner forearm, left hand on the hip.

Walking stance low knife hand block
Gunnun sogi najunde sonkal makgi

Turning to your left, bring your right leg back then place it out behind you to form a left walking stance, using the left hand to form a low knife hand block

Walking stance middle inner forearm block
Gunnun sogi kaunde anpalmok makgi

Stepping forward into a right walking stance, forming a middle side block with the right inner forearm, left hand on the hip.

Walking stance low knife hand block
Gunnun sogi najunde sonkal makgi

Turning to your left, bring your right leg back then place it out behind you to form a left walking stance, using the left hand to form a low knife hand block

Walking stance middle inner forearm block
Gunnun sogi kaunde anpalmok makgi

Stepping forward into a right walking stance, forming a middle side block with the right inner forearm, left hand on the hip.

Parallel ready stance
Narani Junbi Sogi

Bring the right leg back to the left into parallel ready stance.
We now repeat these moves but moving in the opposite direction.

Walking stance low knife hand block
Gunnun sogi najunde sonkal makgi

Taking the left leg back to form a right walking stance, using the right hand to form a low knife hand block, bringing the left hand to the hip.

Walking stance middle inner forearm block
Gunnun sogi kaunde anpalmok makgi

Stepping forward into a left walking stance, forming a middle side block with the left inner forearm, right hand on the hip.

Walking stance low knife hand block
Gunnun sogi najunde sonkal makgi

Turning to your right, bring your left leg back then place it out behind you to form a right walking stance, using the right hand to form a low knife block

Walking stance middle inner forearm block
Gunnun sogi kaunde anpalmok makgi

Stepping forward into a left walking stance, forming a middle side block with the left inner forearm, right hand on the hip.

Walking stance low knife hand block
Gunnun sogi najunde sonkal makgi

Turning to your right, bring your left leg back then place it out behind you to form a right walking stance, using the right hand to form a low knife block

Walking stance middle inner forearm block
Gunnun sogi kaunde anpalmok makgi

Stepping forward into a left walking stance, forming a middle side block with the left inner forearm, right hand on the hip

Walking stance low knife hand block
Gunnun sogi najunde sonkal makgi

Turning to your right, bring your left leg back then place it out behind you to form a right walking stance, using t
he right hand to form a low knife block

Walking stance middle inner forearm block
Gunnun sogi kaunde anpalmok makgi

Stepping forward into a left walking stance, forming a middle side block with the left inner forearm, right hand on the hip

Parallel ready stance
Narani Junbi Sogi

Bring the left leg back to the right into parallel ready stance.

GRADING

You are now ready for your first grading. Grading in Tae Kwon Do is done so that the student can distinguish senior grade from junior grade, black belt from instructor. The grading is reward for hard work, both mentally and physically, that the student has demonstrated over the weeks and months. It cannot be gained purely on a timescale. The student must always be seen to be trying to improve their standard.

For the student to be accepted for promotion, they must -

1. be of the required standard
2. have knowledge of Tae Kwon Do theory.
3. be courteous and respectful to his/her instructor, seniors and fellow students wherever they are.
4. realise that now they are a student of Tae Kwon Do their actions outside the Dojang will reflect on Tae Kwon Do and the instructor.

Tae Kwon Do is a martial art for all ages and sexes and therefore it would be unfair to adopt one grading standard for all students. It is unfair to ask small juniors who have just begun learning English to answer questions in Tae Kwon Do theory. It would be unfair to ask older aged members to perform some of the techniques that the younger students have mastered. This does not mean that the junior and older students will have an easier passage. Juniors may be held at grade longer and older students will be expected to assist more in the class and also have a more extensive knowledge of the Tae Kwon Do theory.

A promotional grading is a formal event and certain points have to be adhered to. If the grading is large there may be long periods of sitting down prior to your test. Students wishing to participate must be able to sit quietly.

At your grading suits *(Doboks)* will be clean and pressed with belts tied correctly. Licences, grading fee and documents will be handed in prior to the exam. There may be a separate payment for the grading which will vary between clubs. Please check with your instructor.

Gradings may take different formats depending on the individual club but here is the format of an Elite grading.

Students will line up and bow to the examiner. The examiner, or instructor, will recite the Tae Kwon Do oath with the students repeating it. Students will then be dismissed to the rear of the class, where they will sit cross-legged until called. When your name is called answer politely, 'present Sir' and go to your designated point on the floor. The number of students demonstrating at any one time will vary from one to a maximum of five,

depending on the size of the grading, the size of the venue and the grade of the student. All techniques that you have to do will be demonstrated by the grading official.
Students will be asked to perform the pattern relevant to their grade and any other pattern that they already know. This may be done as a group or individually, depending on the number of students attending the grading and the size of the venue.

Students will be asked to perform certain stances, hand and kicking techniques. The instructor will demonstrate the technique, the students will follow. Sparring will also be included. The more senior the student, the more technical the moves should be to demonstrate their ability. Senior students may be asked to spar against two opponents at the same time. Breaking will be included for adults only. Junior students may be asked to hold their kick against the board to show correct technique but they will not be asked to break. Senior students will be asked to break to show correct technique and power. Specially made plastic boards are used with different colours denoting the difficulty of the board. The colours we use are white, green, black and brown.

Students are then called forward individually by the examiner and asked questions on theory and the correct naming of techniques. Remember to bow towards the examiner or instructor when approaching them and when walking away.

The examiner will then grade the student and either pass or fail them dependant on their performance at the grading. Once passed, the student can then move onto the next pattern and improve on their techniques and abilities.

We will now look at the patterns of Tae Kwon Do, which are in belt order. Each pattern will have their meaning, descriptions of special moves or moves peculiar to that pattern and the pattern described in detail. When looking at the pattern, it may seem confusing or difficult to follow. These guides are designed to be used in conjunction with attending classes on a regular basis. It may be difficult to learn a new pattern in a class due to the number or complexity of moves. If the class has just had a grading, there may be many students ready to learn a new pattern and the instructor may not have enough time in the class to teach every move in detail. The instructor should ensure that time is spent going over new patterns but ultimately, it may be down to the student to research the pattern to learn the basic moves, the instructor, or senior student, can then refine the pattern in the class.

In these patterns, all photographs are taken from the front. This means that in some moves, only the back is visible. We have therefore included a second picture to show the technique. When 2 photographs are displayed, the left hand one is the move as it occurs in the pattern, the right hand picture is the move and is there for demonstration purposes only.

CHON JI

L stance middle *(niunja sogi)*
When looked at from the front, the feet are almost in a straight line, the feet are a shoulder width apart in length. The front foot faces forward, the rear foot is turned at 90 degrees. Both knees are bent slightly and the weight is distributed 70% on the rear foot, 30% on the front.

Chon Ji literally means "the Heaven the Earth". It is, in the Orient, interpreted as the creation of the world or the beginning of human history, therefore, it is the initial pattern played by the beginner. This pattern consists of two similar parts; one to represent the Heaven and the other the Earth.

Movements – 19

Parallel ready Stance
Narani junbi Sogi

Feet shoulder width apart, toes facing forward. Fists clenched and held level with the belt

Walking stance low outer forearm block
Gunnun sogi najunde bakat palmok makgi

Moving your left foot to the left to form a walking stance whilst executing a low block with the
left forearm.

Walking stance obverse middle punch
Gunnan sogi baro jirugi

Stepping forward with the right foot into walking stance performing a mid section punch with the right hand, left hand on the hip.

Walking stance low outer forearm block
Gunnun sogi najunde bakat palmok makgi

Pivoting on your left foot, turn 180 degrees to face the opposite direction to form a walking stance whilst executing a low block with the right forearm.

Walking stance obverse middle punch
Gunnan sogi baro jirugi

Stepping forward with the left foot into walking stance performing a mid section punch with the left hand, right hand on the hip.

Walking stance low outer forearm block
Gunnun sogi najunde bakat palmok makgi

Moving your left foot, turn to your left to form a walking stance whilst executing a low block with the left forearm.

Walking stance obverse middle punch
Gunnan sogi baro jirugi

Stepping forward with the right foot into walking stance performing a mid section punch with the right hand, left hand on the hip.

Walking stance low outer forearm block
Gunnun sogi najunde bakat palmok makgi

Pivoting on your left foot, turn 180 degrees to face the opposite direction to form a walking stance whilst executing a low block with the right forearm.

Walking stance obverse middle punch
Gunnan sogi baro jirugi

Stepping forward with the left foot into walking stance performing a mid section punch with the left hand, right hand on the hip.

L stance middle inner forearm block
Niunja sogi kaunde anpalmok makgi

Moving your left foot, turn to your left to form an L stance whilst executing a middle block with the left inner forearm.

Walking stance obverse middle punch
Gunnan sogi baro jirugi

Stepping forward with the right foot into walking stance performing a mid section punch with the right hand, left hand on the hip.

L stance middle inner forearm block
Niunja sogi kaunde anpalmok makgi

Pivoting on your left foot, turn 180 degrees to your right to face the opposite direction, forming an L stance whilst executing a middle block with the right inner forearm.

Walking stance obverse middle punch
Gunnan sogi baro jirugi

Stepping forward with the left foot into walking stance performing a mid section punch with the left hand, right hand on the hip.

L stance middle inner forearm block
Niunja sogi kaunde anpalmok makgi

Moving your left foot, turn to your left to form an L stance whilst executing a middle block with the left inner forearm.

Walking stance obverse middle punch
Gunnan sogi baro jirugi

Stepping forward with the right foot into walking stance performing a mid section punch with the right hand, left hand on the hip.

L stance middle inner forearm block
Niunja sogi kaunde anpalmok makgi

Pivoting on your left foot, turn 180 degrees to your right to face the opposite direction, forming an L stance whilst executing a middle block with the right inner forearm.

Walking stance obverse middle punch
Gunnan sogi baro jirugi

Stepping forward with the left foot into walking stance performing a mid section punch with the left hand, right hand on the hip

Walking stance obverse middle punch
Gunnan sogi baro jirugi

Stepping forward with the right foot into walking stance performing a mid section punch with the right hand, left hand on the hip.

Walking stance obverse middle punch
Gunnan sogi baro jirugi

Stepping backward with the right foot into walking stance performing a mid section punch with the left hand, right hand on the hip.

Walking stance obverse middle punch
Gunnan sogi baro jirugi

Stepping backward with the left foot into walking stance performing a mid section punch with the left hand, right hand on the hip.

Parallel ready Stance
Narani junbi Sogi

Feet shoulder width apart, toes facing forward. Fists clenched and held level with the belt.

TENETS OF TAE KWON DO (Tae Kwon Do Jungshin)

Courtesy	*(Ye Ui)*
Integrity	*(Yom Chi)*
Perseverance	*(In Nae)*
Self Control	*(Guk Gi)*
Indomitable Spirit	*(Baekjul Boolgool)*

The Tenets of Tae Kwon Do should serve as a guide for all serious students of the art.

Courtesy *(Ye Ui)*

Tae Kwon Do Students should attempt to practice the following elements of courtesy to build up their noble character and to conduct their training in an orderly manner as well.

1. To be polite to one another
2. To encourage a sense of justice and humanity.
3. To distinguish instructor from student, senior from junior, and eldest from youngest.
4. To promise the spirit of mutual concession.
5. To be ashamed of one's voice, contempting that of others.

Integrity *(Yom Chi)*

In Tae Kwon Do, the word integrity assumes a loose definition than the one usually presented in a dictionary. One must be able to define right from wrong and have the conscience, if wrong, to feel guilt. Listed are some examples where integrity is lacking:

1. The student who requests rank from an instructor, or attempts to purchase it.
2. The student who gains rank for ego purposes or the feeling of power.

Perseverance *(In Nae)*

There is an old oriental saying, *"Patience leads to virtue or merit"- "One can make a peaceful home by being patient 100 times"*. Certainly, happiness and prosperity are most likely to come to the patient person. To achieve something, whether it is a higher degree or the perfection of a technique, one must set a goal then constantly persevere. One of the most important secrets in becoming a leader of Tae Kwon Do is to overcome every difficulty by perseverance

Self Control *(Guk Gi)*

This tenet is extremely important inside and outside the dojang, whenever conducting oneself in free sparring or in one's personal affairs. An inability to live and work within one's capability or sphere is also a lack of self-control. According to Lao-Tzu *"the term of stronger is the person who wins over ones self rather than someone else."*

Indomitable Spirit *(Baekjul Boolgool)*

Indomitable spirit is shown when a courageous person and their principles are pitted against overwhelming odds. A serious student of Tae Kwon Do will at all times be modest and honest. If confronted with injustice, he/she will deal with the belligerent without fear or hesitation at all, with indomitable spirit, regardless of whosoever and however many the number.

TAE KWON DO OATH AND STUDENT RULES

Student Oath

1. I shall observe the tenets of Tae Kwon Do
2. I shall respect my instructors and seniors
3. I shall never misuse Tae Kwon Do
4. I shall be a champion of freedom and justice
5. I shall build a more peaceful world

Students *(Jeja)*

1. Never tire of learning. A good student can learn anywhere, anytime. This is the secret of knowledge.
2. A good student must be willing to sacrifice for his art and instructor. Many students feel that their training is a commodity bought with monthly dues, and are not willing to take part in demonstrations, teaching and working around the Dojang. An instructor can afford to lose this kind of student.
3. Always set a good example to lower ranking belts. It is only natural that they should attempt to emulate senior students.
4. Always be loyal and never criticise the instructor, Tae Kwon Do or the teaching methods.
5. If an instructor teaches a technique, practice and attempt to utilise it.
6. Remember that a student's conduct outside the Dojang reflects on the art and instructor.
7. If a student adopts a technique from another Dojang and the instructor disapproves of it, the student must discard it immediately or train at the gym where the technique was learned.
8. Never be disrespectful to the instructor. Though a student is allowed to disagree, the student must eventually follow the instructor whether he is right or wrong.
9. A student must be eager to learn and ask questions.
10. Never break a trust.

RULES OF THE DOJANG

These rules may differ from club to club but these are the Elite rules. Mostly these are either to show respect to the instructor and senior ranks or general good manners.

1. All students must bow before entering and leaving your training hall or area.
2. Prior to class all students must bow to black belts that enter the hall. This also applies to lower ranking black belts when senior degrees enter. Correct protocol and courtesy must be observed at all times.
3. Always bow before speaking to your instructor
4. At all times, address your instructor as MISTER or SIR, never first names. If the instructor is a lady then MISS is appropriate.
5. No shoes are allowed in the Dojang
6. Raise your hand and request permission before speaking out in class.
7. No idle chatter while training is in progress.
8. When lining up in class, the highest rank is positioned at the right hand side of the front row. Students in succeeding rows should line up directly behind the students in the front row, with the seniority starting from the right hand side.
9. If you arrive late for class, you must first attract the attention of the instructor by raising your hand, approach the instructor, bow and give your reasons.
10. If a student leaves for more than a month, they may be required to take an assessment grading.
11. Uniforms MUST be clean and PRESSED before every training session.
12. If you are on any medication or suffer injury or illness, you must inform the instructor.
13. DO NOT wear jewellery or watches during training.

Along with these rules, general Health and Safety considerations must also be applied. As it is a bare foot art, students must have clean feet with their toe and finger nails trimmed. Bags and other items should be placed at the side of the training area so as not to cause a trip hazard. The instructor should ensure the hall is suitable, that there are no hazards such as loose floor boards or uneven floor and that there is adequate heat and light to allow students to train in a safe and comfortable environment

All Elite instructors are PVG checked (vetted through the Criminal Records Bureau) so that parents of junior students and adult students alike can be sure that they can train in a safe environment.

MOVES SPECIFIC TO DAN GUN

L stance knife hand guarding block
(Niunja sogi sonkal daebi makgi)

This is similar to an outer forearm guarding block but the hands are opened at the point of impact to form a knife hand.

Walking stance high punch (*Gunnun sogi nopunde jirugi*)

This is executed in the same manner as a middle punch but as it is a high section punch, your fist should be at your eye level.

L stance twin forearm block *(Niunja sogi sang palmok makgi)*

A twin forearm block is used to defend against two attacks. A punch from the front and a downward knife hand strike from the side. The hands start about chest level with the hands crossed, knuckles of both hands facing the body. The inner hand twists to the front to form a middle outer forearm block, the hand furthest from the body twists upwards to form a high outer forearm block.

L stance middle knife hand strike
(Niunja sogi kaunde sonkal taerigi)

The hand start about chest level, back fist to back fist. The striking hand is closest to the body. The striking hand is twisted as it comes out to the front, the hand opens at the point of impact. The reaction hand is brought back to the hip and kept clenched. The body is side on to the target.

DAN GUN

Named after the holy Dan-Gun, the legendary founder of Korea in the year 2333 BC.

Movements – 21

	Parallel ready stance *Narani junbi sogi* Feet shoulder width apart, toes facing forward. Hands clenched and held at belt level.
	L stance knife hand guarding block *Niunja sogi sonkal daebi makgi* Turning to your left, perform a left L stance, knife hand guarding block.

Walking stance high punch
Gunnun sogi nopunde jirugi

Stepping forward into a right walking stance, perform a high punch with the right fist.

L stance knife hand guarding block
Niunja sogi sonkal daebi makgi

Pivoting on your left foot, turn to your right to face the opposite direction into a right L stance, knife hand guarding block.

Walking stance high punch
Gunnun sogi nopunde jirugi

Stepping forward into a left walking stance, perform a high punch with the left fist.

Walking stance low outer forearm block
Gunnun sogi najunde bakat palmok makgi

Bring the left leg back to the right, turn to your left placing the left leg in front into a walking stance performing a low section block with the left outer forearm.

Walking stance high punch
Gunnun sogi nopunde jirugi

Stepping forward into a right walking stance, perform a high punch with the right fist.

Walking stance high punch
Gunnun sogi nopunde jirugi

Stepping forward into a left walking stance, perform a high punch with the left fist.

Walking stance high punch
Gunnun sogi nopunde jirugi

Stepping forward into a right walking stance, perform a high punch with the right fist.

L stance twin forearm block
Niunja sogi sang palmok makgi

Pivoting on your front foot, turn anti clockwise in to left L stance performing a twin forearm block

Walking stance high punch
Gunnun sogi nopunde jirugi

Stepping forward into a right walking stance, perform a high punch with the right fist.

L stance twin forearm block
Niunja sogi sang palmok makgi

Pivoting on your left foot, turn to your right to face the opposite direction into a right L stance performing a twin forearm block.

Walking stance high punch
Gunnun sogi nopunde jirugi

Stepping forward into a left walking stance, perform a high punch with the left fist.

Walking stance low outer forearm block
Gunnun sogi najunde bakat palmok makgi

Bring the left leg back to the right, turn to your left placing the left leg in front into a walking stance performing a low section block with the left outer forearm.

Walking stance high outer forearm block
Gunnun sogi nopunde bakat palmok makgi

Remaining in a left walking stance, perform a high outer forearm block with the right forearm.

The previous move and this one are performed in a continuous motion.

Walking stance high outer forearm block
Gunnun sogi nopunde bakat palmok makgi

Stepping forward into a right walking stance, perform a high outer forearm block with the right forearm.

Walking stance high outer forearm block
Gunnun sogi nopunde bakat palmok makgi

Stepping forward into a left walking stance, perform a high outer forearm block with the left forearm.

Walking stance high outer forearm block
Gunnun sogi nopunde bakat palmok makgi

Stepping forward into a right walking stance, perform a high outer forearm block with the right forearm.

L stance middle knife hand strike
Niunja sogi kaunde sonkal taerigi

Pivoting on the right foot, turn to your left to form a let L stance whilst executing a middle outward strike with the left knife hand.

Walking stance high punch
Gunnun sogi nopunde jirugi

Stepping forward into a right walking stance, perform a high punch with the right fist.

L stance middle knife hand strike
Niunja sogi kaunde sonkal taerigi

Pivoting on the right foot, turn to your right to face the opposite direction and form a right L stance whilst executing a middle outward strike with the right knife hand.

Walking stance high punch
Gunnun sogi nopunde jirugi

Stepping forward into a left walking stance, perform a high punch with the left fist.

Parallel ready stance
Narani junbi sogi

Feet shoulder width apart, toes facing forward. Hands clenched and held at belt level.

MOVES SPECIFIC TO DO SAN

Walking stance high outer forearm block
Gunnun sogi nopunde bakat palmok maki

The hands begin about chest level, back fist to back fist with the blocking hand closest to the body. As both hands move, they twist so that the blocking hand is level with the eyes with the outer forearm forming the blocking tool with the arm slightly bent. The reaction hand comes back to the hip, knuckles facing upwards.

Walking stance middle fingertip thrust
Gunnan sogi sonkut tulgi

The reaction hand is used as a blocking tool. The arm starts with the fingers pointing upwards, the elbow bent at 90 degrees. The arm is moved so that the palm of the blocking hand is facing the floor, as if to knock an opponent's punch down wards. The attacking tool is pulled back and then thrust forward, over the top of the blocking hand to strike with the fingertips.

Right hand release

The right hand is twisted sharply anti-clockwise so that the palm faces the floor, both feet come up onto the balls of the feet and are also turned anti-clockwise.
This acts as a release, as if an opponent has grabbed your wrist. The twist must be sharply so that it releases the grip on your wrist.

Walking stance wedging block
Gunnan sogi hechyo makgi

Both hands are lifted level with the face, with both back fists facing away from you. Both hands are rotated outwards so that they finish level with your eyes, blocking with both outer fore arms. This is to block a double punch to the face.

DO SAN

Is the pseudonym of the patriot Ahn Chang-Ho (1876-1938) The 24 movements' represent his entire life, which he devoted to furthering the education of Korea and its independence movement.

Movements – 24

Parallel ready Stance.
Narani junbi Sogi

Feet shoulder width apart, toes facing forward. Fists clenched and held level with the belt.

Walking stance high outer forearm block
Gunnun sogi nopunde bakat palmok maki

Move the left foot to face the left forming a left foot walking stance. Execute a high section outer forearm block with the left hand, bringing the right hand back to the hip.

Walking stance middle reverse punch
Gunnun sogi kaunde bande jirugi

Perform a right hand mid-section reverse punch whilst maintaining a left walking stance

Walking stance high outer forearm block
Gunnun sogi nopunde bakat palmok maki

Turning clockwise, move the right foot to face the opposite direction, forming a left right walking stance. Execute a high section outer forearm block with the right hand, bringing the left hand back to the hip.

Walking stance middle reverse punch
Gunnun sogi kaunde bande jirugi

Perform a left hand mid-section reverse punch whilst maintaining a right walking stance

L stance knife hand guarding block
Niunja sogi sonkal daebi makgi

Turning to your left, perform a left L stance, knife hand guarding block.

Walking stance middle fingertip thrust
Gunnan sogi sonkut tulgi

Stepping forward into a right walking stance, executing a middle fingertip thrust with the right hand.

Right hand release

The right hand is twisted sharply anti-clockwise so that the palm faces the floor, both feet come up onto the balls of the feet and are also turned anti-clockwise.

Walking stance high back fist strike
Gunnan Sogi nopunde dung joomuk

After the release, turn anti-clockwise 180 degrees into a left walking stance, performing a high back fist strike with the left hand, the right hand coming back to the hip.

Walking stance high back fist strike
Gunnan Sogi nopunde dung joomuk

Step forward into a right walking stance, performing a high back fist strike with the right and, the left hand coming back to the hip.

Walking stance high outer forearm block
Gunnun sogi nopunde bakat palmok maki

Pivoting on the right foot, turn anti-clockwise 90 degrees, forming a left foot walking stance. Execute a high section outer forearm block with the left hand, bringing the right hand back to the hip.

Walking stance middle reverse punch
Gunnun sogi kaunde bande jirugi

Perform a right hand mid-section reverse punch whilst maintaining a left walking stance

Walking stance high outer forearm block
Gunnun sogi nopunde bakat palmok maki

Turning clockwise, move the right foot to face the opposite direction, forming a left right walking stance. Execute a high section outer forearm block with the right hand, bringing the left hand back to the hip.

Walking stance middle reverse punch
Gunnun sogi kaunde bande jirugi

Perform a left hand mid-section reverse punch whilst maintaining a right walking stance

Walking stance high wedging block
Gunnan sogi nopunde hechyo makgi

Pivoting on the right foot, turn 135 degrees to your left forming a left walking stance, high section wedging block.

Front snap kick
Apcha busigi

Perform a front snap kick with the right foot, keeping your hands is the wedging block position

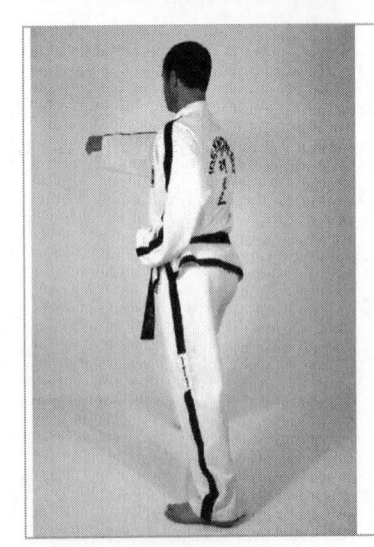

Walking stance middle obverse punch
Gunnan sogi baro jirugi

Placing the right foot down into a walking stance, perform a right mid section punch with the right hand.

Walking stance middle reverse punch
Gunnan sogi bandae jirugi

Remaining in a right walking stance perform a left mid section punch. This move and the previous move are carried out in fast motion.

Walking stance high wedging block
Gunnan sogi nopunde hechyo makgi

Pivoting on the left foot, turn 45 degrees to your right forming a right walking stance, high section wedging block.

Front snap kick
Apcha busigi

Perform a front snap kick with the left foot, keeping your hands in the wedging block position.

Walking stance middle obverse punch
Gunnan sogi baro jirugi

Placing the left foot down into a walking stance, perform a left mid section punch with the left hand.

Walking stance middle reverse punch
Gunnan sogi bandae jirugi

Remaining in a left walking stance perform a right mid section punch. This move and the previous move are carried out in fast motion.

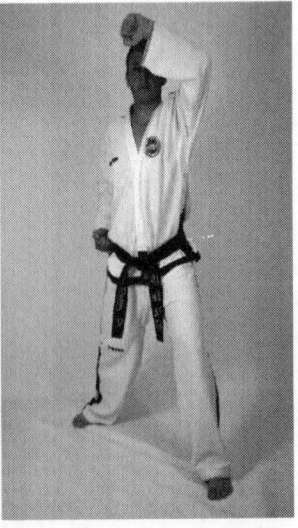

Walking stance rising block
Gunnan sogi chookyo makgi

Lifting the left leg, place it so that you are travelling in a direct line back to your starting point, forming a walking stance, using the left arm to form a rising block.

Walking stance rising block
Gunnan sogi chookyo makgi

Walking forward, form a right walking stance using the right arm to form a rising block.

Sitting stance middle side strike
Annun sogi kaunde yop taerigi

Pivoting on the right foot, turn anti-clockwise to form a sitting stance, left knife-hand side strike.

Sitting stance middle side strike
Annun sogi kaunde yop taerigi

Bring your left leg to your right leg then step out to the right to form a sitting stance, right knife-hand side strike.

Parallel ready Stance.
Narani junbi Sogi

Bring your right foot back to ready stance.

As Tae Kwon Do is a Korean martial art, then students must have an understanding of Korean. Instructors may give instructions in class in both English and Korean, to help students understand the terminology. When attending a grading, students may be asked to name various terms they have learned or are relevant to that level of grading. This section lists the basic Korean terms then shows you how to form a command.

As all the relevant stances, blocks and strikes are pictured within the various pattern explanations, they are not pictured here.

Stances *(Sogi)*

Ready stance →	Junbi sogi
Attention stance →	Charyot sogi
Sitting stance →	Annun sogi
Walking stance →	Gunnun sogi
L stance →	Niunja sogi
Bending stance →	Guburyo sogi
X stance →	Kyocha sogi
Close ready stance →	Moa junbi sogi

(There are four types of close ready stance – A, B, C and D)

Hand parts *(Sang Bansin)*

Fore fist →	Ap Joomuk
Back fist →	Dung Joomuk
Side fist →	Yop Joomuk
Palm →	Sonbadak
Knife hand	Sonkal
Reverse Knife hand →	Sonkal Dung
Flat Fingertip →	Opun Sonkut
Straight Fingertip →	Sun Sonkut
Backhand →	Sondung

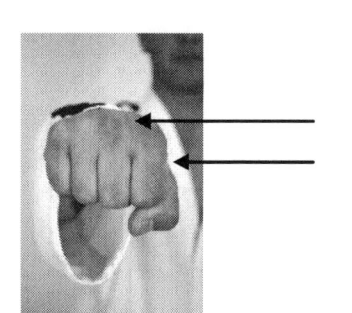

With both the punch and back fist, only the first two knuckles are used.

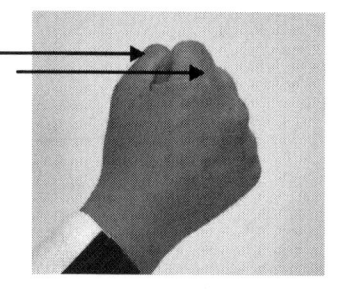

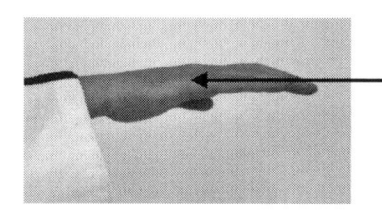

Knife hand uses the outer edge of the hand

Reverse knife hand uses the thumb side of the hand.

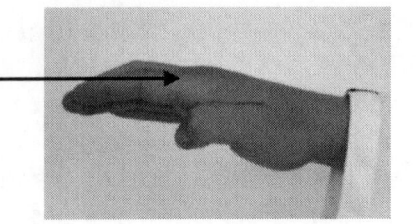

Arm parts →
- Front Elbow → Ap Palkup
- Outer Forearm → Bakat Palmok
- Inner Forearm → An Palmok

Foot parts *(Habansin)* →
- Ball of Foot → Ap Kumchi
- Footsword → Balkal
- Back Heel → Dwichook
- Instep → Baldung

Instep
Back heel
Ball of foot
Footsword

ATTACKING TECHNIQUES *(Gong Gyoki)*

A PUNCH *(Jirugi)* is used primarily to cause an internal haemorrhage rather than surface damage by twisting the attacking tool.

A THRUST *(Tulgi)* is delivered with the intention to cut through the vital spot with less twisting of the attacking tool.

A STRIKE *(Taerigi)* is used to destroy or break the bone or muscles of vital spots with the least twist of the attacking tool.

KICKING TECHNIQUES

Front snap kick⟶ Ap Chagi Busigi
Turning kick⟶ Dollyo Chagi
Side piercing kick⟶ Yop Cha Jirugi
Back piercing kick⟶ Dwitcha chagi
Reverse turning kick⟶ Bandae Dollyo Chagi
Reverse hooking kick⟶ Bandae Golcho Chagi
Flying kick⟶ Twimyo Chagi

When constructing these terms into a command or instruction, it follows the same format.

stance ⟶ what stance is to be used

height or level ⟶ the intended height (low, middle, high)

part of tool to be used ⟶ what part of the arm is used for blocking, or what part of the hand etc is to be used.

The technique to be used ⟶ blocking or attacking tool

To put this into a command, it would look like this:

L stance⟶low⟶outer forearm⟶block
niunja sogi⟶najunde⟶bakat palmok⟶makgi

walking stance⟶high⟶obverse⟶punch
gunnun sogi⟶nopunde⟶baro⟶jirugi

(with this move, the obverse section could be missed out as you would do an obverse punch unless told otherwise)

sitting stance ⟶middle⟶knife hand⟶strike
annun sogi⟶kaunde⟶sonkal⟶taerigi

With kicking techniques, only the height and kick are given, you will be told what stance and hand technique to use after the kick.

Middle→turning kick
Kaunde→dollyo chagi

High→side piercing kick
Nopunde→yopcha jirugi

COUNTING IN KOREAN

1 *hanah*
2 *dool*
3 *set*
4 *net*
5 *dasot*
6 *yasot*
7 *ilgop*
8 *yadol*
9 *ahop*
10 *yool*

MOVES SPECIFIC TO WON HYO

L stance high inwards knife hand strike
(Niunja sogi nopunde sonkal anuro taerigi)

This strike uses the knife hand and is aimed at a target to the front and slightly to the side. The hand starts out to the side of the body and is brought towards the centre of the body. The hand is clenched and opened at the moment of impact. The reaction hand starts out at the opposite side of the body and is brought to the opposite shoulder.

Fixed stance middle punch (*Gojung sogi kaunde jirugi*)

A fixed stance is similar to an L stance but slightly longer.
There should be 1 ½ shoulder widths between the front toes and inside edge (the same side as the big toe) of the rear foot. The body weight is spread evenly on both legs. When executing the middle punch in this stance, it is important to bring the striking hand back to the shoulder then punched straight out towards the target. The reaction hand is brought up to the centre of the body then pulled back to the hip.

Walking stance inner forearm circular block *(Gunnun sogi anpalmok dollimyo makgi)*

This block uses a circular motion to scoop and opponents kick or punch away. The knees are bent to drop the body slightly, the blocking hand drops down, comes across the front of the knee and brought back up in an anti-clockwise circular motion to scoop away an attacking tool. The body is half facing, with the blocking shoulder forward.

Low front snap kick *(Najunde apcha busigi)*

This kick is aimed at an attacker directly in front. The kicking area is the ball of the foot, remember to pull the toes back. The kicking leg is raised and the knee is pulled up towards the chest, the foot is then kicked out. The standing foot should be pointing forwards at the moment of impact. The standing leg should be slightly bent.

WON HYO

The noted monk who introduced Buddhism to the Silla Dynasty in the year 686 AD

Movements – 28

Close ready stance A
Moa junbi sogi A

Left hand over the right fist, about eye level, feet together, body upright.

L stance twin forearm block
Niunja sogi sang palmok makgi

Move the left foot to the left to form an L stance, executing a twin forearm block.

L stance high inwards knife hand strike
Niunja sogi nopunde sonkal anuro taerigi

Keeping the feet in a left L stance, perform a high section inward knife hand strike with the right hand, bringing the left hand back to the right shoulder.

Fixed stance middle punch
Gojung sogi kaunde jirugi

Moving the left foot into a fixed stance, perform a middle punch with the left hand, bringing the right hand back to the hip.

L stance twin forearm block
Niunja sogi sang palmok makgi

Move the left foot to the right, then move the right foot out to the right to form an L stance, executing a twin forearm block.

L stance high inwards knife hand strike
Niunja sogi nopunde sonkal anuro taerigi

Keeping the feet in a right L stance, perform a high section inward knife hand strike with the left hand, bringing the right hand back to the left shoulder.

Fixed stance middle punch
Gojung sogi kaunde jirugi

Moving the right foot into a fixed stance, perform a middle punch with the right hand, bringing the left hand back to the hip.

Bending ready stance A
Guburyo junbi sogi A

Bring the right foot to the left, turn to face forward, bringing the left foot up, executing a guarding block with the hands.

Middle side piercing kick
Kaunde yopcha jirugi

Execute a middle section side piercing kick with the left foot, punching the left hand out over the kick.

L stance guarding block
Niunja sogi sonkal daebi makgi

Lower the left foot into a left L stance, executing a knife hand guarding block.

L stance guarding block
Niunja sogi sonkal daebi makgi

Stepping forward into a right L stance, executing a knife hand guarding block.

L stance guarding block
Niunja sogi sonkal daebi makgi

Stepping forward into a left L stance, executing a knife hand guarding block.

Walking stance middle fingertip thrust
Gunnan sogi sonkut tulgi

Stepping forward into a right walking stance, executing a middle fingertip thrust with the right hand.

L stance twin forearm block
Niunja sogi sang palmok makgi

Pivoting on the right foot, turn anti-clockwise to form a left L stance executing a twin forearm block with the hands.

L stance high inwards knife hand strike
Niunja sogi nopunde sonkal anuro taerigi

Keeping the feet in a left L stance, perform a high section inward knife hand strike with the right hand, bringing the left hand back to the right shoulder.

Fixed stance middle punch
Gojung sogi kaunde jirugi

Moving the left foot into a fixed stance, perform a middle punch with the left hand, bringing the right hand back to the hip

L stance twin forearm block
Niunja sogi sang palmok makgi

Move the left foot to the right, then move the right foot out to the right to form an L stance, executing a twin forearm block.

L stance high inwards knife hand strike
Niunjas sogi nopunde sonkal anuro taerigi

Keeping the feet in a right L stance, perform a high section inward knife hand strike with the left hand, bringing the right hand back to the left shoulder.

Fixed stance middle punch
Gojung sogi kaunde jirugi

Moving the right foot into a fixed stance, perform a middle punch with the right hand, bringing the left hand back to the hip.

Walking stance circular block
Gunnun sogi anpalmok dollimyo makgi

Bringing the right foot to the left, step forward into a left walking stance whilst executing a circular block with the right inner forearm.

Low front snap kick
Najunde apcha busigi

Execute a low front snap kick with the right foot, keeping the hands in the circular block position.

Walking stance middle reverse punch
Gunnun sogi kaunde bandae jirugi

Place the right foot down into a right walking stance, executing a middle punch with the left hand, bringing the right hand back to the hip.

Walking stance circular block
Gunnun sogi anpalmok dollimyo makgi

Execute a circular block with the left inner forearm.

Low front snap kick
Najunde apcha busigi

Execute a low front snap kick with the left foot, keeping the hands in the circular block position.

Walking stance middle reverse punch
Gunnun sogi kaunde bandae jirugi

Place the left foot down into a left walking stance, executing a middle punch with the right hand, bringing the left hand back to the hip.

Bending ready stance A
Guburyo junbi sogi A

Bringing the right foot forward into the left knee to form a bending ready stance, executing a guarding block with the hands.

Middle side piercing kick
Kaunde yopcha jirugi

Execute a middle section side piercing kick with the right foot, punching the right hand out over the kick.

L stance middle outer forearm guarding block
Niunja sogi kaunde bakat palmok daebi makgi

Placing the right foot down and pivot clockwise to your left to form a left L stance, outer forearm guarding block.

L stance middle outer forearm guarding block
Niunja sogi kaunde bakat palmok daebi makgi

Bring the left foot into the right then move the right foot out into an L stance, executing an outer forearm guarding block with the hands.

Close ready stance A
Moa junbi sogi A

Bring the right foot back to a close ready stance A.

MOVES SPECIFIC TO YUL GOK

Sitting stance *(Annun sogi)*

The first movement is carried out in slow motion and is designed to measure the distance to your target. As you start to move your foot to the left, form a left punch level with the right shoulder line. As your foot moves to the left, move your punch horizontally to the left. As your foot stops, your punch should be level with your left shoulder. The reaction hand is clenched and pulled to the opposing hip.

Walking stance middle hooking block
(*Gunnun sogi kaunde golcho makgi*)

Walking stance middle hooking block
(*Gunnun sogi kaunde golcho makgi*)

Walking stance middle punch
(*Gunnun sogi kaunde baro jirugi*)

These three moves are easier described when taken in sequence from the pattern. The first hooking block with the right palm is half facing. The palm is open and is used to block an attacker punch by grabbing the back of the fist, therefore, the fingers should be angled to the side slightly so that the area between the thumb and forefinger is facing forward. The block starts with the hands chest level, hands back fist to back fist, blocking hand closest to the body. The block is similar to an outer forearm block but with the hand opening to block.

The second hooking block is done on the spot with the opposite hand. Again, this is half facing but as it is the reverse hand, the opposite shoulder is forward this time. The rear foot should come up onto the ball of the foot so that the heel is raised off the ground. The punch is then executed in fast motion, dropping the rear heel to the ground.

Bending ready stance A
(*Guburyo junbi sogi*)

This stance is primarily used to prepare for a side kick. The standing leg is bent slightly and the foot is turned to face the side, the kicking leg is bent and brought up so that it is level with the standing knee. The bent knee should be facing towards the target, in this case, forwards. The hands are in a guarding block. When standing on the right leg, it is a right bending stance.

Walking stance front elbow strike
Gunnun sogi ap palkup taerigi)

This strike uses the front elbow. The striking hand should be brought up to the shoulder, the elbow is then brought forward horizontally to strike. The reaction hand is taken out to the front, as if grabbing an opponent by the back of the neck. The hand then pulls the opponent onto the strike. When the elbow strikes the open palm, the fingers should be level with the elbow with the palm resting along the forearm.

L stance twin knife hand block
(Niunja sogi sang sonkal makgi)

This knife hand block is similar to a twin forearm block but the hands are opened at the point of impact to form a knife hand. The hands start chest level with both knuckles facing the body, the rising hand closest to the body. The rising hand twists to block an attack to the head from the side. The other hand forms a block to the front. Both blocks should reach their targets at the same time.

X stance high back fist side strike
(Kyocha sogi nopunde dung joomuk yop taerigi)

This stance is formed after a jump, landing on the front foot, the rear foot bent, crossing over the rear of the standing leg. The front leg should be bent slightly with most of the body weight. The rear foot rests on the ball. If the right leg is the standing foot, then it is a right X stance. The back fist strike begins with both hands chest level, back fist to back fist, striking hand closest to the body.

YUL GOK

The pseudonym of the great philosopher and scholar YI I (1536-1584) nicknamed the 'Confucius of Korea'. The 38 movements of the pattern refer to his birthplace on 38° latitude and the diagram represents 'Scholar'.

Movements – 38

	Parallel ready Stance *Narani junbi Sogi* Feet shoulder width apart, toes facing forward. Fists clenched and held level with the belt.
	Sitting stance *Annun sogi* Move the left foot to the left to form a sitting stance. Extend the left fist to shoulder line.

Sitting stance middle punch
Annun sogi kaunde jirugi

Keeping the feet in a sitting stance perform a middle punch with the right hand, bringing the left back to the hip.

Sitting stance middle punch
Annun sogi kaunde jirugi

Keeping the feet in a sitting stance perform a middle punch with the left hand, bringing the right back to the hip.

These two punches are performed in fast motion.

Sitting stance
Annun sogi

Move the left foot to the right then move the right foot to the right to form a sitting stance. Extend the right fist to shoulder line.

Sitting stance middle punch
Annun sogi kaunde jirugi

Keeping the feet in a sitting stance perform a middle punch with the left hand, bringing the right back to the hip.

Sitting stance middle punch
Annun sogi kaunde jirugi

Keeping the feet in a sitting stance perform a middle punch with the right hand, bringing the left back to the hip.

These two punches are performed in fast motion

Walking stance middle outer forearm block
Gunnun sogi kaunde bakat palmok makgi

Moving the right foot 45 degrees to your right, form a right walking stance whilst executing a middle outer forearm block with the right forearm.

Low front snap kick
Najunde apcha busigi

Keeping the hands in the block position, perform a low front snap kick with the left foot.

Walking stance middle punch
Gunnun sogi kaunde baro jirugi

Place the left foot down into a walking stance whilst performing a middle punch with the left hand

Walking stance middle punch
Gunnun sogi kaunde bandae jirugi

Keeping the feet in a left walking stance, perform a middle punch with the right hand.

These two punches are performed in fast motion.

Walking stance middle outer forearm block
Gunnun sogi kaunde bakat palmok makgi

Moving the left foot to form a 45 degrees to your left, forming a left walking stance whilst executing a middle outer forearm block with the left forearm.

Low front snap kick
Najunde apcha busigi

Keeping the hands in the block position, perform a low front snap kick with the right foot.

Walking stance middle punch
Gunnun sogi kaunde baro jirugi

Place the right foot down into a walking stance whilst performing a middle punch with the right hand.

Walking stance middle punch
Gunnun sogi kaunde bandae jirugi

Keeping the feet in a right walking stance, perform a middle punch with the left hand.

These two punches are performed in fast motion

Walking stance middle hooking block
Gunnun sogi kaunde golcho makgi

Moving the right foot, form a right walking stance to the front whilst executing a hooking block with the right palm.

Walking stance middle hooking block
Gunnun sogi kaunde golcho makgi

Keeping the feet in a walking stance perform a hooking block with the left palm.

Walking stance middle punch
Gunnun sogi kaunde baro jirugi

Keeping the feet in a walking stance perform a middle punch with the right hand.

The above hooking block and this punch are performed in a connecting motion motion.

Walking stance middle hooking block
Gunnun sogi kaunde golcho makgi

Moving the left foot forward, form a right walking stance to the front whilst executing a hooking block with the left palm.

Walking stance middle hooking block
Gunnun sogi kaunde golcho makgi

Keeping the feet in a walking stance perform a hooking block with the right palm.

Walking stance middle punch
Gunnun sogi kaunde baro jirugi

Keeping the feet in a walking stance perform a middle punch with the left hand.

The above hooking block and this punch are performed in a connecting motion.

Walking stance middle punch
Gunnun sogi kaunde baro jirugi

Stepping forward into a right walking stance, middle punch with the right hand.

Bending ready stance A
Guburyo junbi sogi

Bringing the left leg forward, form a right bending ready stance A with the hands in a guarding block position.

Middle side piercing kick
Kaunde yopcha jirugi

Execute a middle side piercing kick with the left leg, punching the right hand out above the kick.

Walking stance front elbow strike
Gunnun sogi ap palkup taerigi

Place the left foot down into a left walking stance whilst executing a front elbow strike with the right elbow.

Bending ready stance A
Guburyo junbi sogi

Pivoting on the left leg, turn to face the rear to form a left bending ready stance A with the
hands in a guarding block position.

Middle side piercing kick
Kaunde yopcha jirugi

Execute a middle side piercing kick with the right leg, punching the left hand out above the kick.

Walking stance front elbow strike
Gunnun sogi ap palkup taerigi

Place the right foot down into a left walking stance whilst executing a front elbow strike with the left elbow.

L stance twin knife hand block
Niunja sogi sang sonkal makgi

Bring your left leg forward then turn to your left, placing the left foot out into an L stance, forming a twin knife hand block.

Walking stance middle fingertip thrust
Gunnan sogi sonkut tulgi

Stepping forward into a right walking stance, execute a middle fingertip thrust with the right hand.

L stance twin knife hand block
Niunja sogi sang sonkal makgi

Pivoting on the left foot, turn to face the opposite direction forming a right L stance. Execute a twin knife hand block.

Walking stance middle fingertip thrust
Gunnan sogi sonkut tulgi

Stepping forward into a left walking stance, execute a middle fingertip thrust with the left hand.

Walking stance high outer forearm block
Gunnun sogi nopunde bakat palmok makgi

Bringing your left foot back, turn to face the rear and place it out to form a left walking stance, high outer forearm block with the left forearm.

Walking stance middle punch
Gunnun sogi kaunde bandae jirugi

Keeping the feet in a left walking stance, perform a middle punch with the right hand.

Walking stance high outer forearm block
Gunnun sogi nopunde bakat palmok makgi

Stepping forward, form a right walking stance, high outer forearm block with the right forearm.

Walking stance middle punch
Gunnun sogi kaunde bandae jirugi

Keeping the feet in a right walking stance, perform a middle punch with the left hand.

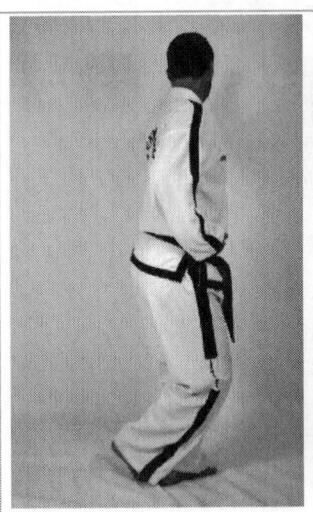

X stance high back fist side strike
Kyocha sogi nopunde dung joomuk yop taerigi

Jumping forward, land in a left X stance, executing a high side strike with the left back fist.

Walking stance double forearm block
Gunnun sogi doo palmok makgi

Pivoting on the left foot, turn clockwise and form a right walking stance, executing a double forearm block.

Walking stance double forearm block
Gunnun sogi doo palmok makgi

Bring the right foot to the left, turn to face the opposite direction and place your left foot out into a walking stance, executing a double forearm block.

Parallel ready Stance
Narani junbi Sogi

Bring the left foot back to parallel ready stance.

MISCELLANEOUS TERMS AND DEFINITIONS

In Tae Kwon Do, there are numerous terms used with the various moves to indicate height, attacking or blocking point, stance, how to move. This section will cover the more commonly used terms to give you a better understanding of the moves and patterns.

High section *(Nopunde)*

Middle section *(Kaunde)*

Low section *(Najunde)*

When carrying out a high section move, the blocking or attacking tool is in line with your own eye, it is always in relation to your own height. High section in a ready stance (as above) is higher than a high section when in a low stance. Similarly, when facing a taller opponent, high section is level with your own eye level but chest level on your opponent. This would not make it a middle section as it level with your own eye level. Middle and low sections are the same in that the height is in relation to your own body.

The body is also divided laterally into:
A - shoulder line   B - Chest line   C - Solar plexus line

A B C

These points are used with attacking and blocking hand techniques:

Full facing (left), the shoulders are level.

Half facing (right), the shoulder of the blocking tool is slightly further forward than the reaction shoulder.

Obverse punch (left)
The punching hand is the same as the leading leg

Reverse punch (right)
The punching hand is the opposite of the leading leg.

Upward and downward movements are self explanatory. Inward and outward movements are moves that are to the side. An inward movement starts out at the side of the body and finishes near the centre of the body. An outward movement starts near the centre of the body and moves away from the body, finishing at the side.

When moving, there are various way to do this, depending on the technique or stance used. The most widely used method is stepping. This is moving forward a step at a time and can be forward, backwards or to the side.
If you are in a right walking stance, for example, to move to a left walking stance, you would move the left leg forward, taking a step. If moving backward, the right leg is moved back. There is no difference if the technique is full or half facing. If you were in a side facing technique, for example, a sitting stance and you wanted to move to the left, you would either bring the right leg to meet the left, place it down, then move the left leg to the

side. Alternatively, you could bring the right foot and cross it over the left, then move the left foot out into a sitting stance.

There are various ways to turn around to face an attacker. The most commonly used are pivoting and spot turning. Pivoting is turning on the ball of the foot to face the intended direction. It can be done on either the front or back foot, depending on the stance or technique. Spot turning can be done either clockwise or anti-clockwise. We will described the clockwise version as follows:

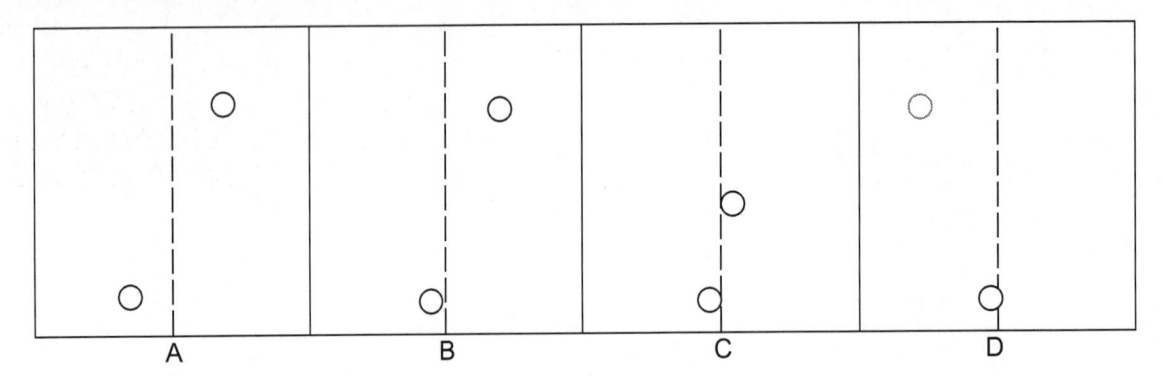

In the above diagram, it shows the 4 stages of spot turning. The circles represent the feet, the dotted line is the centre line between the feet. The circle at the bottom of the box is the leading foot in a walking stance, in this example, the right foot.

A – this represent a right walking stance
B – the right foot is lifted and placed near to the centre line
C – the left foot is brought forwards and into the centre line
D – turn your body to face the opposite direction, placing the left foot out into a walking stance.

This turn can be done in numerous stances but always follows the same sequence of movements.

MOVES SPECIFIC TO JOONG GUN

Rear foot stance palm upward block *(Dwitbal sogi sondabak ollyo makgi)*

With a rear foot stance, the front foot faces forward, the rear foot is turned to face the side. The feet are 1 shoulder width apart between the toes. Both knees are bent slightly and are above the toes. Most of the body weight is on the rear foot, the front foot only touches the ground with the ball of the foot. If the left foot is at the rear then it is a left rear foot stance.

Walking stance upper elbow strike
(Gunnun sogi wi palkup taerigi

This is used to strike an opponent under the chin with an elbow. The moves starts with the arm bent, the fist almost touching the shoulder with the elbow facing the floor. The elbow is then brought straight up so that the wrist finishes next to your ear with the elbow facing forward. The reaction hand starts out to the front of the body and is pulled back to the hip.

Walking stance twin upset punch
(Gunnun sogi sang dwijibun jirugi)

This punching technique is used against two attackers who are standing side by side to your front. Both hands are pulled back to the hips then punched forward, both forearms parallel to the ground. Both hands are angled outwards slightly.

Walking stance X fist rising block
(*Gunnun sogi kyocha joomuk chookyo makgi*)

A rising block is used to defend against an opponents downward strike. Both hands start about chest level and are then punched upwards, crossing over to finish with the wrists just above eye level.

L stance high back fist side strike *(Niunja sogi nopunde dung joomuk taerigi)*

Walking stance release

Walking stance high punch *(Gunnun sogi nopunde bande jirugi)*

These 3 moves are best described in sequence as they appear in the pattern. The first picture shows a high back fist strike. The hands start as if doing an outer forearm block but the hand is twisted so that the back fist is outward, to strike an opponent to the temple. The second move, the release, is used as if your opponent has grabbed your back fist. Raise your body slightly, lifting your reaction hand up to about chest level then drop your body weight, pull your reaction hand quickly back to the hip and twist your grabbed hand sharply downwards so that the back fist is facing the ground. Using fast motion, perform a high punch with your opposite hand.

Low stance pressing block *(Nachuo sogi sondabak noollo makgi)*

low stance is similar to walking stance but the stance is longer by one foot. The pressing block is used to push an opponents attack, normally a front kick, downwards. The hands starts about shoulder level with the hand closed, the hand is opened as it moves downwards to about belt level. The hand should be opened at the point of impact. The hand should be turned slightly so that the pinkie is facing the opponent. The reaction hand starts extended towards the ground then it moves upwards, the hand also finishes open.

Fixed stance U shape block *(Gojung sogi digutja makgi)*

This sole purpose of this block is to block a pole or similar object. An opponent would attempt to strike with a pole held straight up and down, the block is used to catch the pole between the thumb and fore finger of each hand. The hands start about chest level and are pushed across the body. The lower elbow should finish on the hip, the top arm about eye level.

JOONG GUN

Named after the patriot Ahn Joong-Gun who assassinated Hiro-Bumi Ito, the first Japanese governor-general of Korea who played the leading part in the Korea-Japan merger. There are 32 movements in this pattern to represent Mr Ahns age when he was executed at Lui-Shung prison in 1910.

Movements – 32

Close ready stance B
Moa junbi sogi B

Feet are together and body upright. The right hand is held in the left and hands are held out to the front about belt level.

L stance middle reverse knife hand block
Niunja sogi kaunde sonkal dung makgi

Move the left foot to the left to form an L stance executing a middle block using a reverse knife hand with the left hand.

Low side front snap kick
Najunde yobap cha busigi

Using the left leg perform a low side front snap kick, keeping the hands in the same position.

Rear foot stance palm upward block
Dwitbal sogi sondabak ollyo makgi

Stepping forward to form a left rear foot stance whilst performing an upward block with the right palm.

L stance middle reverse knife hand block
Niunja sogi kaunde sonkal dung makgi

Pivoting on the left foot, turn to face the opposite direction into a right L stance executing a middle block using a reverse knife hand with the right hand.

Low side front snap kick
Najunde yobap cha busigi

Using the right leg perform a low side front snap kick, keeping the hands in the same position.

Rear foot stance palm upward block
Dwitbal sogi sondabak ollyo makgi

Stepping forward to form a right rear foot stance whilst performing an upward block with the left palm.

L stance middle knife hand guarding block
Niunja sogi sonkal daebi makgi

Moving the left foot, turn to your left to form a left L stance, middle knife hand guarding block

Walking stance upper elbow strike
Gunnun sogi wi palkup taerigi

Stepping forward into a left walking stance perform an upwards elbow strike with the right elbow, bringing the left hand back to the hip.

L stance middle knife hand guarding block
Niunja sogi sonkal daebi makgi

Stepping forward into a right L stance middle knife hand guarding block

Walking stance upper elbow strike
Gunnun sogi wi palkup taerigi

Stepping forward into a right walking stance perform an upwards elbow strike with the left elbow, bringing the right hand back to the hip.

Walking stance high vertical twin fist punch
Gunnun sogi nopunde sang joomuk

Stepping forward into a right walking stance perform a twin vertical punch.

Walking stance twin upset punch
Gunnun sogi sang dwijibun jirugi

Stepping forward into a right walking stance, executing a twin upset punch to the front.

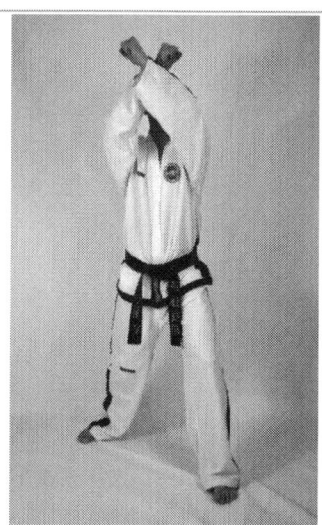

Walking stance X fist rising block
Gunnun sogi kyocha joomuk chookyo makgi

Pivoting on the right foot, turn to face the rear into a left walking stance performing a rising block with the X fist.

L stance high back fist side strike
Niunja sogi nopunde dung joomuk taerigi

Lift your left foot, turn to the left into a left L stance performing a high side strike with the left back fist.

Walking stance release

Lifting the left foot, slide it into a left walking stance. Twist your left hand so that the back fist is facing the ground

Walking stance high punch
Gunnun sogi nopunde bande jirugi

Remaining in a left walking stance execute a high punch with the right hand.

The above movement and this one are execute in a fast motion

L stance high back fist side strike
Niunja sogi nopunde dung joomuk taerigi

Bring your left foot to the right, then move your right foot to form a right L stance performing a high side strike with the right back fist.

Walking stance release

Lifting the right foot, slide it into a left walking stance. Twist your right hand so that the back fist is facing the ground

Walking stance high punch
Gunnun sogi nopunde bande jirugi

Remaining in a left walking stance execute a high punch with the left hand.

The above movement and this one are execute in a fast motion.

Walking stance high double forearm block
Gunnun sogi nopunde doo palmok makgi

Bringing the right foot into the left, turn to the rear and form a left walking stance, executing a high section double forearm block.

L stance middle punch
Niunja sogi kaunde jirugi

Moving the left foot, form a left L stance executing a middle punch with the left hand.

Middle side piercing kick
Kaunde yopcha jirugi

Perform a middle side piercing kick with the right foot whilst executing a high punch with the right hand.

Walking stance high double forearm block
Gunnun sogi nopunde doo palmok makgi

Place the right foot down into a walking stance, executing a high section double forearm block.

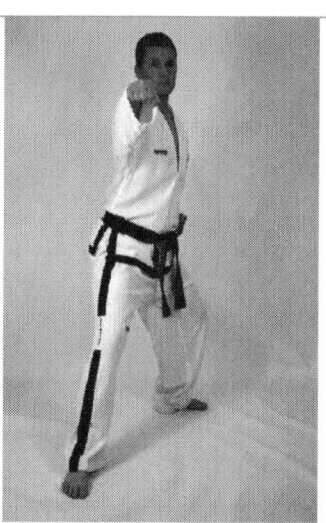

L stance middle punch
Niunja sogi kaunde jirugi

Moving the right foot, form a right L stance executing a middle punch with the right hand.

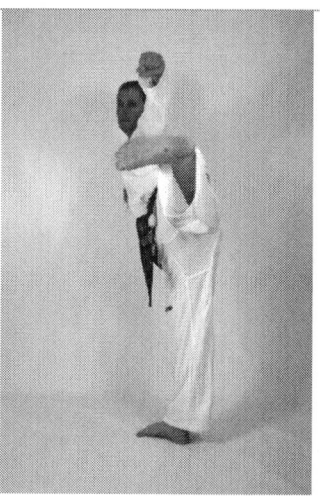

Middle side piercing kick
Kaunde yopcha jirugi

Perform a middle side piercing kick with the left foot whilst executing a high punch with the left hand.

L stance middle forearm guarding block
Niunja sogi kaunde palmok daebi makgi

Place the left foot down into an L stance, executing a middle forearm guarding block.

Low stance pressing block
Nachuo sogi sondabak noollo makgi

Moving the left foot into a low stance, executing a palm pressing block with the right palm.

This is done in slow motion.

L stance middle forearm guarding block
Niunja sogi kaunde palmok daebi makgi

Stepping forward into an L stance, executing a middle forearm guarding block.

Low stance pressing block
Nachuo sogi sondabak noollo makgi

Moving the right foot into a low stance, executing a palm pressing block with the leftt palm.

This is done in slow motion.

Close stance angle punch
Moa sogi giokja jirugi

Bring the left foot into the right to form a close stance. Perform an angle punch with the right hand.

This is done in slow motion.

Fixed stance U shape block
Gojung sogi digutja makgi

Move the right foot forward into a fixed stance, executing a U shape block

Fixed stance U shape block
Gojung sogi digutja makgi

Bring the right foot to the left, then move the left foot to the left into a fixed stance, executing a U shape block

Close ready stance B
Moa junbi sogi B

Bring the left foot back into a Close ready stance B.

MOVES SPECIFIC TO TOI GYE

Walking stance low upset fingertip thrust
(Gunnun sogi najunde dwijibun sonkut tulgi)

With the thrust, the striking hand is brought up to the shoulder then thrust downwards, in a straight line, the target being the groin area. The hand is clenched and opens at the point of impact, palm facing upwards. The reaction hand is extended out then pulled sharply inwards to the opposite shoulder.

Close stance side back strike
(Moa sogi yopdwi taerigi)

This strike uses the back fist and is used against an attacker who is standing behind and slightly to the side. Both hands start at the opposite side of the body, the striking hand is brought up so that the back fist is used to strike, it is important that the elbow is in line with the fist, not in front of it. The opposite hand is used as a reaction hand and is extended to the front.

Sitting stance W shape block
(Annun sogi san makgi)

A W shape block can be used to defend against either 1 or 2 attackers executing a high technique and uses either the forearm or knife hand. The forearm is used in this pattern. The block is either full or half facing, depending on the stance used, this is sitting stance so it is full facing. The foot is stamped down to accentuate the hip motion to assist with power. The foot is only stamped down when defending against 1 opponent. The hands start in a W shape and remain there until the point of impact.

Walking stance high flat fingertip thrust
(Gunnun sogi opun sonkut tulgi)

This fingertip thrust is executed the same as a middle punch but the hand is opened at the point of impact to strike with the fingertips, the open palm facing the floor. The reaction hand is clenched and is brought back to the hip.

X stance, X fist pressing block
(*Kyocha sogi kyocha joomuk makgi*)

An X stance is normally used to attack the front or side in a jumping motion. The majority of the weight is on the front foot, the other foot crosses over behind, resting on the ball of the foot. If the weight is on the right foot, it is a right X stance.
The jumping motion prior to landing is used as if jumping over a small obstacle, not for achieving distance.

Walking stance circular block
(*Gunnun sogi dollimyo makgi*)

This block uses a circular motion to scoop and opponents kick or punch away. The knees are bent to drop the body slightly, the blocking hand drops down, comes across the front of the knee and brought back up in an anti-clockwise circular motion to scoop away an attacking tool. The body is half facing, with the blocking shoulder forward.

TOI GYE

The pen name of the noted scholar Yi Hwang (16th century), an authority on neo-Confucianism. The 37 movements of the pattern refer to his birthplace on 37° latitude and the diagram represents 'Scholar'.

Movements – 37

Close ready stance B
Moa junbi sogi B

Feet together, Body upright, right hand clenched in the left hand.

L stance middle inner forearm block
Niunja sogi kaunde anpalmok makgi

Moving the left foot, turn to your left to form an L stance whilst executing an middle inner forearm block with the left hand, bringing the right back to the hip.

Walking stance low upset fingertip thrust
Gunnun sogi najunde dwijibun sonkut tulgi

Moving the left foot to form a walking stance, perform a low upset fingertip thrust with the right hand, bringing the left hand back to the shoulder.

Close stance side back strike
Moa sogi yopdwi taerigi

Bring the left leg into the right to form a close stance. The right hand executes a side back strike whilst the left hand is extended to the front.

This is done in slow motion.

L stance middle inner forearm block
Niunja sogi kaunde anpalmok makgi

Moving the right foot, turn to your right to form an L stance whilst executing an middle inner forearm block with the right hand, bringing the left back to the hip.

Walking stance low upset fingertip thrust
Gunnun sogi najunde dwijibun sonkut tulgi

Moving the right foot to form a walking stance, perform a low upset fingertip thrust with the left hand, bringing the right hand back to the shoulder.

Close stance side back strike
Moa sogi yopdwi taerigi

Bring the right leg into the left to form a close stance. The left hand executes a side back strike whilst the right hand is extended to the front.

This is done in slow motion.

Walking stance X fist pressing block
Gunnun sogi kyocha joomuk noollo makgi

Stepping forward with the left leg into a walking stance, performing a pressing block with an X fist.

Walking stance high twin fist vertical punch
Gunnun sogi nopunde sang joomuk sewo jirugi

Keeping the feet in a walking left walking stance perform a high vertical twin fist punch to the front.

Middle front snap kick
Kaunde apcha busigi

Keeping the hands in the same position, perform a middle front snap kick with the right foot.

Walking stance middle punch
Gunnun sogi kaunde jirugi

Placing the right foot down into a right walking stance, perform a middle punch with the right fist.

Walking stance middle punch
Gunnun sogi kaunde jirugi

Keeping the feet in a right walking stance, perform a middle punch with the left fist.

Close stance twin side elbow
Moa sogi sang yop palkup

Bringing the left leg into the right to form a close stance. Both fists are brought to the sides at belt level with the elbows thrust out to the side.

This is done in slow motion.

Sitting stance W shape block
Annun sogi san makgi

Lifting the right foot, turn clockwise to face the rear, stamping the right foot down into a sitting stance whilst performing a W shape block with both hands.

Sitting stance W shape block
Annun sogi san makgi

Lifting the left foot, turn anti-clockwise to face the front, stamping the left foot down into a sitting stance whilst performing a W shape block with both hands.

Sitting stance W shape block
Annun sogi san makgi

Lifting the left foot, turn clockwise to face the rear, stamping the left foot down into a sitting stance whilst performing a W shape block with both hands.

Sitting stance W shape block
Annun sogi san makgi

Lifting the right foot, turn anti-clockwise to face the front, stamping the right foot down into a sitting stance whilst performing a W shape block with both hands.

Sitting stance W shape block
Annun sogi san makgi

Lifting the left foot, turn clockwise to face the rear, stamping the left foot down into a sitting stance whilst performing a W shape block with both hands.

Sitting stance W shape block
Annun sogi san makgi

Lifting the left foot, turn clockwise to face the front, stamping the left foot down into a sitting stance whilst performing a W shape block with both hands.

L stance low double forearm pushing block
Niunja sogi najunde doo palmok miro makgi

Bring the right foot into the left then step forward with the left to form an L stance whilst performing a double forearm pushing block.

Walking stance head grab

Moving the left foot into a walking stance, extend both hands upwards as if grabbing an opponent's head.

Knee upward kick
Moorup ollyo chagi

Bringing the right leg forward, execute an upward kick with the knee whilst pulling both hands downwards.

L stance middle knife hand guarding block
Niunja sogi kaunde sonkal daebi makgi

Lower the right foot next to the left, turn anti-clockwise to face the rear and step forward into a right L stance. Perform a middle knife hand guarding block with the hands.

Low side front snap kick
Najunde yobap cha busigi

Raise the left foot and perform a low side front snap kick, keeping the hands in the guarding block position.

Walking stance high flat fingertip thrust
Gunnun sogi opun sonkut tulgi

Place the left foot down into a walking stance, executing a high flat fingertip thrust with the left hand, the right is clenched and brought back to the hip.

L stance middle knife hand guarding block
Niunja sogi kaunde sonkal daebi makgi

Stepping forward into a right L stance, perform a middle knife hand guarding block with the hands.

Low side front snap kick
Najunde yobap cha busigi

Raise the right foot and perform a low side front snap kick, keeping the hands in the guarding block position.

Walking stance high flat fingertip thrust
Gunnun sogi opun sonkut tulgi

Place the right foot down into a walking stance, executing a high flat fingertip thrust with the right hand, the left is clenched and brought back to the hip.

L stance side back strike
Niunja sogi yopdwi taerigi

Moving the right foot backwards, form a left L stance. The right hand performs a side back strike using the back fist. The left hand forms a low block.

X stance, X fist pressing block
Kyocha sogi kyocha joomuk makgi

Jumping forward, land on the right foot, crossing the left behind it. Form a pressing block with the X fist.

Walking stance high double forearm block
Gunnun sogi nopunde doo palmok makgi

Stepping forward with the right foot into a walking stance whilst executing a double forearm block.

L stance low knife hand guarding block
Niunja sogi najunde sonkal daebi makgi

Pivoting on the right foot, turn anti-clockwise to form a left L stance, low knife hand guarding block.

Walking stance circular block
Gunnun sogi dollimyo makgi

Move the left foot to form a walking stance whilst executing a circular block with the right hand, the left is brought back to the hip.

L stance low knife hand guarding block
Niunja sogi najunde sonkal daebi makgi

Bring the left foot into the right, then move the right foot to form a an L stance, low knife hand guarding block

Walking stance circular block
Gunnun sogi dollimyo makgi

Move the right foot to form a walking stance whilst executing a circular block with the left hand, the right is brought back to the hip.

Walking stance circular block
Gunnun sogi dollimyo makgi

Keeping your feet in roughly the same spot, turn to form a walking stance in the opposite direction whilst executing a circular block with the right hand, the left is brought back to the hip.

Walking stance circular block
Gunnun sogi dollimyo makgi

Keeping your feet in roughly the same spot, turn to form a walking stance in the opposite direction whilst executing a circular block with the left hand, the right is brought back to the hip.

Sitting stance middle punch
Annun sogi jirugi

Move the right foot to form a sitting stance whilst executing a middle punch with the right hand.

Close ready stance B
Moa junbi sogi B

Bring the right foot into the left. Feet together, Body upright, right hand clenched in the left hand.

POWER

Tae Kwon Do is a powerful art if practised and used correctly. Power is achieved by the following elements being used. If any of these elements are missing then power will also be missing.

Concentration *(Jip Joong)*

Whether it is an attacking or defensive technique, the power should be concentrated onto the smallest part of the blow. If you were to use the whole fist to punch, the power would be spread over a large area and lessen the blow. If the power is concentrated into a smaller area, the first two knuckles only, then there is more power being delivered by the strike.

Equilibrium *(Kyun Hyung)*

Good balance is essential to deliver the correct technique. If the body weight is incorrectly spread or balance is not maintained when moving, full power cannot be achieved.

Breath Control *(Hohup Jojul)*

Correct breathing can either assist the student to deliver a powerful technique or condition the body to receive a blow. By exhaling sharply at the point of impact, helps to tense the body to deliver a blow.

Mass *(Zilyang)*

By using maximum speed and mass, we can increase the power delivered by a blow. By raising the body slightly as the start of a movement then dropping the body weight at the moment of impact will deliver a powerful blow. This is also known as sine wave.

Speed *(Sokdo)*

By delivering a blow with speed, scientifically, force = mass x speed. To assist with speed, we can use reaction to assist. If we were to punch with our right hand, we can pull the left hand back to the hip, the quicker it's pulled back the more speed can be generated.

Middle obverse punch
(baro jirugi)

This is a punch to the centre of the body. The striking hand is brought back to the hip with the knuckles facing upwards. The other hand (reaction hand) is brought out to the front, knuckles facing the floor. As the punch is extended, the reaction hand is brought sharply back to the hip. Both hands twist so that the punch finishes knuckles facing the floor and the reaction hand ends on the hip, knuckles facing upwards. The body is upright and the shoulders are full facing.

You will recognise the above explanation from the white belt booklet. As a senior belt, the above technique should be done with power. This is done in various ways, depending on the stance or type of technique but will all use sine wave. This is the use of dropping your body weight at the point of impact, which, combined with the other aspects, will greatly improve the amount of power generated in the movement.

When moving forward to punch, the student raises their body slightly and extends the reaction hand. As the leading leg moves forward, the body drops slightly, the reaction hand is brought sharply back to the hip, the punching hand is extended equally as fast, twisting the hands as they do so. As the leading leg stops, the body drops and the punch is fully extended to strike the target.

If the punch is done whilst static, the student should drop their body slightly by bending the knees, the body is raised by straightening the legs then dropped at the moment of impact, the feet do not move.

If the punch is part of a continuous movement, 2 moves in quick succession, the body does not drop, the rear leg is raised slightly, coming up onto the ball of the foot, which raises the body. The foot is then dropped back down at the moment of impact, dropping the body slightly.

Low outer forearm block
(*najunde bakat palmok makgi*)

This is a low section block using the outer forearm (the part of the forearm on the pinkie side of the hand). The block starts with both hands crossed, level with the chest, the blocking hand closest to the body. The blocking hand has the knuckles facing the body and the reaction hand has the knuckles facing away from the body (back fist to back fist). As the blocking hand is brought down, the hand twists so that the hand finishes with the knuckles facing the floor. The arm is bent slightly and the body is upright, half facing.

This explanation for a low outer forearm block is again taken from the white belt booklet. To generate maximum power, the sine wave principles, as described above, are used. However, as this block is half facing, the hip can be twisted to assist. If this block is done whilst moving forward, the body is twisted slightly in the opposite direction of the intended block. As the student moves forward the principles of sine wave are used, along with the hip movement. If the block is done whilst static, the hips can still be used but to as lesser degree. This allows the block to be used with maximum force.

It should also be noted that when executing a block or strike, the attacking or blocking tool used should be brought form the start position to the finish position in the most direct route. For instance, if you are performing a punch in a walking stance, the punching hand is on the hip and the reaction hand is extended. The punching hand should be moved directly from the hip to the point of impact. Similarly, the reaction hand should be also brought back to the hip in a straight line.

MOVES SPECIFIC TO HWA RANG

Sitting stance middle pushing block
(Annun sogi kaunde sondabak miro makgi)

The arm is extended outward in line with the shoulder. The hand is opened so that the palm is used as the blocking tool, the reaction hand is on the hip.

L stance upward punch
(Niunja sogi ollyo jirugi)

The attacking arm is brought backwards then forward and up in a circular motion. The reaction hand is extended outwards then brought sharply back to the opposite shoulder. The back fist is kept facing the front at the point of impact. This is used to punch an opponent on the chin at close range.

Vertical stance knife hand downward strike
(Soojik sogi sonkal naeryo taerigi)

In vertical stance the body is upright and half facing, the legs are straight. The feet are in the same position as an L stance but they are one shoulder with apart from big toe to big toe. 60% body weight is on the rear foot and 40% on the front foot. When the right foot is at the rear it is a right vertical stance and vice versa.

For the knife hand downward strike, the attacking arm is lowered to the front of the body then raised towards the opposite shoulder then over the head in a large circular motion to the point of impact.

In the left picture, the left hand is used to grab an opponent's punch. The right hand is used to simulate this. As the side kick is extended, the left hand is pulled backwards, this would pull an opponent forward onto the kick, allowing you to deliver more force as the opponent cannot move away from the kick.

L stance middle punch
(Niunja sogi kaunde jirugi)

This punch is delivered in L stance and uses the rear arm. As with walking stance, the reaction arm is extended, the punching hand is brought back to the hip. As the punch is extended, the reaction hand is brought back to the hip. The target area is about 1 foot width to the left of the front foot for a left hand punch. Similarly, a right hand punch is about 1 foot width to the right of the front foot. The body remains half facing at the point of impact.

L stance side elbow thrust
(Niunja sogi yop palkup tulgi)

This elbow thrust is delivered by sliding the rear foot into an L stance. In this example, only the right elbow is used to strike, the left arm is used as a reaction arm. Both arms are extended outwards to the front, both arms are brought back at the same time so that both hands stop about belt level. As only 1 elbow is striking, you look at your target area.

Close stance side front block

(Moa sogi yobat makgi)

In this block, only the raised hand is a blocking tool, the opposite hand being a reaction hand. In this picture, the hands start in the opposite position (the blocking hand is facing downward, the reaction hand facing upward). Keeping the elbows stationary, rotate both arms so that they cross over in front of the body. The blocking tool stops so that it is level with the shoulder, the reaction hand stops about belt level.

HWA RANG

Named after the Hwa-Rang youth group which originated in the Silla Dynasty in the early 7th century. The 29 movements refer to the 29th Infantry Division where Tae Kwon-Do developed into maturity.

Movements – 29

Close ready stance C
Moa junbi sogi C

Feet are together and facing forward, hands are open with the left hand on top of the right, about belt level. The middle finger nail of the left hand should sit on top of the middle fingernail of the right hand.

Sitting stance middle pushing block
Annun sogi kaunde sondabak miro makgi

Move the left foot into a walking stance, executing a palm pushing block with the left hand, right hand on the hip.

Sitting stance middle punch
Annun sogi kaunde jirugi

Remaining in sitting stance perform a middle punch with the right hand, left hand pulled back to the hip.

Stance middle punch
Annun sogi kaunde jirugi

Remaining in sitting stance perform a middle punch with the left hand, right hand pulled back to the hip.

L stance twin forearm block
Niunja sogi sang palmok makgi

Lifting the right foot, turn to the right and form an L stance, arms forming a twin outer forearm block.

L stance upward punch
Niunja sogi ollyo jirugi

Remaining in L stance, perform an upward punch with the left hand, pulling the right hand into the left shoulder.

Fixed stance middle punch
Gojung sogi kaunde jirugi

Lifting the right foot, form a fixed stance, executing a middle punch with the right hand, pulling the left hand back to the hip.

Vertical stance knife hand downward strike
Soojik sogi sonkal naeryo taerigi

Pulling the right foot back into a vertical stance, execute a downward strike with the right knife hand, pulling the left hand back to the hip.

Walking stance middle obverse punch
Gunnun sogi baro jirugi

Stepping forward with the left leg into a walking stance, executing a middle obverse punch with the left hand, right hand pulled back to the hip.

Walking stance low outer forearm block
Gunnun sogi najunde bakat palmok makgi

Pivoting on the left leg, turn to your left and form a left walking stance, low outer forearm block with the left hand.

Walking stance middle obverse punch
Gunnan sogi baro jirugi

Stepping forward with the right foot into walking stance performing a mid section punch with the right hand, left hand on the hip.

Shift the left foot forward slightly, bringing the right fist into the left palm.

Middle side piercing kick
Kaunde yopcha jirugi

Raising the right leg, execute a middle side kick with the right foot, pulling both hands backwards.

L stance middle knife hand outward strike
Niunja sogi kaunde sonkal bakuro taerigi

Placing the right foot down into an L stance, perform an ouward strike with the right knife hand.

Walking stance middle obverse punch
Gunnun sogi baro jirugi

Stepping forward with the left leg into a walking stance, executing a middle obverse punch with the let hand, right hand pulled back to the hip.

Walking stance middle obverse punch
Gunnun sogi baro jirugi

Stepping forward with the right leg into a walking stance, executing a middle obverse punch with the right hand, left hand pulled back to the hip.

L stance middle knife hand guarding block
Niunja sogi sonkal daebi makgi

Pivoting on the right foot, turn anti clockwise to face what was your right into an L stance, middle guarding block with the knife hand.

Walking stance middle fingertip thrus
Gunnan sogi sonkut tulgi

Stepping forward into a right walking stance, executing a middle fingertip thrust with the right hand, the left hand being used as a blocking tool.

L stance middle knife hand guarding block
Niunja sogi kaunde sonkal daebi makgi

Turning to face the opposite direction, form a left L stance whilst executing a middle guarding block with the knife hand.

High turning kick
Nopunde dollyo chagi

Moving forward, perform a high turning kick with the right foot

High turning kick
Nopunde dollyo chagi

Lifting the left leg, perform a high turning kick
(the above two kicks are performed in fast motion)

L stance middle knife hand guarding block
Niunja sogi kaunde sonkal daebi makgi

Place the left foot down to form a left L stance whilst executing a middle guarding block with the knife hand.

Walking stance low outer forearm block
Gunnun sogi najunde bakat palmok makgi

Pivoting on the right foot, turn to face the rear into a right walking stance whilst executing a low block with the right outer forearm.

L stance middle punch
Niunja sogi kaunde jirugi

Moving the left foot, slide it to form a left L stance whilst performing a middle punch with the right hand.

L stance middle punch
Niunja sogi kaunde jirugi

Stepping forward into a right L stance whilst performing a middle punch with the left hand.

L stance middle punch
Niunja sogi kaunde jirugi

Stepping forward into a left L stance whilst performing a middle punch with the right hand.

Walking stance X fist pressing block.
Gunnun sogi kyocha joomuk makgi

Bringing the left foot back slightly, move it forwards into a left walking stance, executing a pressing block with the X fist.

L stance side elbow thrust
Niunja sogi yop palkup tulgi

Stepping forward, slide the right foot into an L stance whilst performing a side elbow thrust with the right elbow.

Close stance side front block
Moa sogi yobat makgi

Pivoting on the right foot, turn anti clockwise to form a close stance whilst executing a side front block with the right hand, the left hand extended downward.

Close stance side front block
Moa sogi yobat makgi

Remaining in a close stance, perform a side front block with the left hand, extending the right hand downward.

L stance middle knife hand guarding block
Niunja sogi kaunde sonkal daebi makgi

Move the left foot forward to form a left L stance whilst executing a middle guarding block with the knife hand.

L stance middle knife hand guarding block
Niunja sogi kaunde sonkal daebi makgi

Move the left foot to the right to form a right L stance whilst executing a middle guarding block with the knife hand.

Close ready stance C
Moa junbi sogi C

Feet are together and facing forward, hands are open with the left hand on top of the right, about belt level. The middle finger nail of the left hand should sit on top of the middle fingernail of the right hand.

MOVES SPECIFIC TO CHOONG MOO

Walking stance high knife hand strike
(Gunnun sogi nopunde sonkal taerigi)

This strike start with the attacking tool held out to the side of the body, hand clenched. It is brought towards the centre of the body, stopping level with the shoulder, opening the hand at the point of impact. The left hand is a reaction hand and is not used as a block.

Flying side piercing kick *(Twimyo yopcha jirugi*

As with all side kicks, the sword edge of the foot is used, the non-kicking leg is tucked up under the kicking leg. The hand is extended to form a punch with the reaction hand pulled back.

Walking stance head grab

Both hands are brought up about neck height and about head width apart. The hands are open with palms facing the floor, the thumbs are extended out. As this is done in walking stance, the body is slightly lower and there is a tendency for a student to reach up to where an opponent's neck would be if they were standing upright. The grab should be in line with your own neck/head.

Upward knee kick *(Ollyo chagi)*

This strike with the knee is aimed at the chest or solar plexus. By pulling an opponents head downward, it brings the chest into a position that can be struck with the knee, by keeping hold of the head during the strike, it stops your opponent from pulling away as the strike is delivered

A move not pictured is the 360 degree jump turn between the U shape block and landing in guarding stance. To execute the move, jump up directly from the L stance, the higher you get your knees, the easier the move. Turn your body anti clockwise. As you are about to land, allow your hands to travel past the
guarding block position so that as you place your feet down, you can execute a guarding block, rather than just placing your hands in the position.

150

Sitting stance middle front block
(Annun sogi kaunde ap makgi)

This block uses the outer forearm. The block starts with the hand brought up to the side, about shoulder level, knuckles facing forward. The reaction hand is extended out to the front of the body. The blocking hand is brought across the body, twisting as it moves to stop in line with the centre of the body, knuckles facing you. The reaction hand is pulled sharply to the hip.

L stance knife hand checking block
(Niunja sogi kyocha sonkal)

Both hands start at the side of the body, about shoulder level, hands clenched. The hands are then brought downwards, across the body, opening the hands at the point of impact.

Walking stance palm upward block
(Gunnun sogi sang sonbadak ollyo makgi)

Both hands start at the side of the body, about belt level, hands clenched. Both hands are moved away from the body, in a circular motion, outwards and downwards to drop below the belt then as they are brought upwards the hands open to form the block.

CHOONG MOO

The name given to the great Admiral Yi Soon Sin of the Lee Dynasty. He was reputed to have invented the first armoured battleship, Kobukson, in 1592, which is said to be the precursor of the present day submarine. The reason why this pattern ends with a left hand attack is to symbolise his regrettable death, having no chance to show his unrestrained potentiality checked by the forced reservation of his loyalty to the king.

Movements – 30

	Parallel ready stance *Narani junbi sogi* Feet shoulder width apart, toes facing forward. Hands clenched and held at belt level.
	L stance twin knife hand block *Niunja sogi sang sonkal makgi* Stepping to your left form a left L stance whilst executing a twin knife hand block

Walking stance high knife hand strike
Gunnun sogi nopunde sonkal taerigi

Stepping forward form a right walking stance whilst executing a high section knife hand strike with the right hand brining the left hand in front of your forehead.

L stance middle knife hand guarding block
Niunja sogi sonkal daebi makgi

Pivoting on the left foot, turn anti clockwise to face the opposite direction forming a right L stance, arms forming a knife hand guarding block.

Walking stance high fingertip thrust
Gunnun sogi nopunde sonkut tulgi

Stepping forward into a left walking stance, the right hand performing a high fingertip thrust, bringing the right hand back to the hip.

L stance middle knife hand guarding block
Niunja sogi sonkal daebi makgi

Pivoting on the right foot, turn to your left forming a left L stance, arms forming a knife hand guarding block.

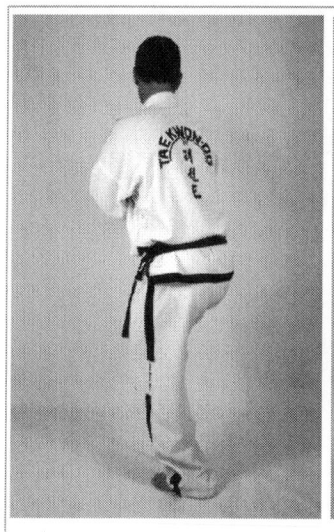

Right bending ready stance A
Guburyo junbi sogi A

Coming up onto the left leg, turn to face the rear forming a bending ready stance.

Middle side piercing kick
Kaunde yopcha jirugi

Perform a middle side piercing kick with the right foot, executing a high punch with the right hand.

L stance middle knife hand guarding block
Niunja sogi sonkal daebi makgi

Placing the right foot down, turn to face the front to form a left L stance, arms forming a knife hand guarding block.

Flying side piercing kick
Twimyo yopcha jirugi

Stepping forward, jump to execute a flying side piercing kick with the right foot.

L stance middle knife hand guarding block
Niunja sogi sonkal daebi makgi

Land forming a right L stance, arms forming a knife hand guarding block.

L stance low outer forearm block
Niunja sogi najunde bakat palmok makgi

Pivoting on the right foot, turn anti clockwise to form a left L stance, executing a low block with the left outer forearm.

Walking stance head grab

Moving the left foot into a walking stance, raise both hands as if grabbing an opponents head.

Upward knee kick
Ollyo chagi

Raising the right knee into an upward kick whilst pulling both hands downward.

Walking stance high reverse knife hand strike
Gunnun sogi nopunde sonkal dung taerigi

Placing the right foot next to the left foot, pivot on the right foot, turn to face the opposite direction, placing the left foot forward into a walking stance, perform a high strike with the right reverse knfie hand, the left hand is brought in under the right elbow.

High turning kick
Nopunde dollyo chagi

Perform a high turning kick with the right leg., then place the right foot next to the right foot.

Middle back piercing kick
Kaunde dwitcha jirugi

Raising the left leg, perform a back piercing kick then place the foot down next to the right foot

L stance middle outer forearm guarding block
Niunja sogi kaunde bakat palmok makgi

Stepping forward with the right foot into an L stance, performing a middle guarding block with the inner forearm.

Middle turning kick
kaunde dollyo chagi

Perform a middle turning kick with the left leg, then place it down next to the right foot.

Fixed stance U shape block
Gojung sogi digutja makgi

Stepping forward with the right foot (towards your stating position) form a fixed stance, the arms executing a U shape block,

L stance middle knife hand guarding block
Niunja sogi kaunde sonkal daebi kakgi

Jump and spin 360 degrees anti clockwise, land in a right L stance, executing a middle guarding block with the knife hand.

Walking stance low upset fingertip thrust
Gunnun sogi najunde dwijibo sonkut

Stepping forward into a left walking stance, performing a low, upset fingertip thrust with the right hand.

L stance side back strike, low outer forearm block
Niunja sogi yop taerigi, najunde bakat palmok makgi

Keeping your feet in roughly the same position, form a left L stance. Execute a side back strike with the right hand whilst executing a low block with the left outer forearm.

Walking stance middle fingertip thrust
Gunnun sogi kaunde sonkut tulgi

Stepping forward into a right walking stance, perform a middle fingertip thrust with the right hand.

Walking stance high double forearm block
Gunnun sogi nopunde doo palmok makgi

Turning anti clockwise, pivoting on the right foot, place the left foot down into a walking stance, executing a high block with the double forearm.

Sitting stance middle front block
Annun sogi kaunde ap makgi

Bring the right foot around to face your left into a sitting stance. Perform a middle front block with the right hand.

Sitting stance high back fist side strike
Annun sogi nopunde dung joomuk yop taerigi

Remaining in a sitting stance, perform a high side strike with the right back fist. The previous move and this one are done consecutively.

Middle side piercing kick
Kaunde yopcha jirugi

Pivoting on the left foot, perform a middle side piercing kick with the right foot then place it down next to the left foot.

Middle side piercing kick
Kaunde yopcha jirugi

Perform a middle side piercing kick with the left foot then place it down next to the right foot, turning to face the opposite direction.

L stance knife hand checking block
Niunja sogi kyocha sonkal

Step forward with the right foot into an L stance, performing an X-knife hand checking block.

Walking stance palm upward block
Gunnun sogi sang sonbadak ollyo makgi

Stepping forward into a right walking stance, executing an upward block with the twin palm.

Walking stance high outer forearm block
Gunnun sogi nopunde bakat palmok makgi

Turning to face the opposite direction into a right walking stance, executing a high outer forearm block with the right hand.

Walking stance middle reverse punch
Gunnun sogi bandae jirugi

Remaining in a walking stance execute a middle reverse punch with the left hand.

Parallel ready stance
Narani junbi sogi

Feet shoulder width apart, toes facing forward. Hands clenched and held at belt level.

Printed in Great Britain
by Amazon